THE CATHOLIC UNIVERSITY OF AMERICA
CANON LAW STUDIES
No. 242

The Privilege of the Canon

A HISTORICAL SYNOPSIS AND COMMENTARY

BY

REV. JAMES McGRATH, B.A., J.C.L.
Priest of the Archdiocese of Philadelphia

A DISSERTATION

Submitted to the Faculty of the School of Canon Law of the Catholic University of America in Partial Fulfillment of the Requirements for the Degree of Doctor of Canon Law

THE CATHOLIC UNIVERSITY OF AMERICA PRESS
WASHINGTON, D. C.
1946

Nihil Obstat:

Eduardus G. Roelker, S.T.D., J.C.D.,

Censor Deputatus.

Washingtonii, die 22 julii 1946.

Imprimatur:

✠ D. Card. Dougherty,

Archiepiscopus Philadelphiensis.

Philadelphiae, die 25 julii 1946.

The Walther Printing House
Philadelphia

TO MY MOTHER

TABLE OF CONTENTS

CANONICAL COMMENTARY

CHAPTER VI

CHAPTER VII

FOREWORD

Although the legal principles governing the canonical institute known as "The Privilege of the Canon" are succinctly contained in the Code of Canon Law in canons 119 and 2343, nevertheless this term as such is not to be found therein. One might, therefore, be led to conclude that in the course of time the term has perhaps been indiscriminately appended to this legislation by some author or authors as a means of classification. Almost everyone who has ever proposed to write at any length on the subject of canon law has stated — although perhaps he has not couched it in just so many precise words — that the study of a law together with its historical background will clarify and in some manner explain the law as it is found in its present form. Many of the juridical principles are more clearly understood and their mutual relationship becomes more patent after an analysis of their history has disclosed the main lines and trends of development, for the formation of ecclesiastical law, excluding the divine law, is influenced to a great extent by the contingencies of place and time. With regard to the juridic institute in question, it can be stated at this point without proof that the present term "Privilege of the Canon" has a historical basis.

Christ instituted His Church as an organization or unequal society consisting of clergy and laymen, and He entrusted the government and guidance of it to the former, i. e., to bishops, priests, and other ministers. The threefold power of teaching, ruling and sanctifying the faithful was conferred on the Apostles and their successors. In a word, clergymen were to have a position of preeminence and were to rule and direct the laity to the attainment of their eternal destiny. The laity consequently were obliged to show respect, reverence and obedience to the clergy in proportion, of course, to their varying grades and offices. This serves as the legal basis for the clerical prerogative later known as the "Privilege of the Canon."

The privilege itself was formally incorporated in the body of Canon Law in the year 1139 when, under Pope Innocent II

(1130-1143), the II General Council of the Lateran issued the famous canon *"Si quis suadente diabolo."* Through the enactment of this canon a censure of excommunication was *ipso facto* incurred by those who violated the person of a clergyman or a monk. Within a short span of time this penalty was referred to by the canonists of the time as "the excommunication of the canon," and the protection afforded by the enactment of this canon was simply put within the category of clerical privileges and immunities.

In the present work the main purpose of the first part is to indicate the historical background which prompted the issuance of the canon, and then to point out the main trends in its evolution up to the publication of the Code of Canon Law. In order to give a fuller explanation of the law as it existed in the *Corpus Iuris Canonici,* it is deemed advisable to include a few remarks on the development prior to the legislation of the II General Council of the Lateran.

Substantially, although with some modifications and additions, the law of the II General Council of the Lateran is reiterated in the Code of Canon Law. The second part of this work, then, is devoted to a canonical commentary on the current law.

The writer takes this occasion to extend a sincere expression of gratitude to His Eminence, Dennis Cardinal Dougherty, Archbishop of Philadelphia, for the opportunity of advanced study in Canon Law; to the members of the Faculty of the School of Canon Law for their scholarly direction and valuable assistance; and to all others who contributed by their interest and aid towards the completion of this dissertation.

CHAPTER I

NON-CANONICAL SOURCES

Article 1 — Origin in Ecclesiastical Law

Although the privilege of the canon was not formally incorporated in the body of Church law until the twelfth century, it was known before that time. But no matter how far back one may go in one's attempt to see traces of this prerogative, it cannot be maintained that it is one of the clerical rights or privileges stemming from divine law.[1] It must rather be maintained that the privilege was first observed as a custom by means of the respect which the laity showed to the clergy, and after many decades of customary observance it found its way into positive ecclesiastical legislation. Perhaps the greatest argument in behalf of this tenet lies in the fact that it has never been controverted and has received the unanimous support of all authors.[2]

The only argument which seems to militate against this view is a statement from the Council of Tribur (895), which mentioned that the bishop was to use his canonical authority to see that just compensation be made to a cleric who had suffered any real injury "contrary to divine and human laws."[3] To adduce

1 Ferraris, *Prompta Bibliotheca, Canonica, Iuridica, Moralis, Theologica, necnon Ascetica, Polemica, Rubricistica, Historica* (8 vols., Romae, 1885-1892, Vol. IX ed. I. Bucceroni, Romae, 1899), II, 316, s. v. "clericus," art. II, n. 85 (hereinafter cited *Bibliotheca)*; Maupied, *Juris Canonici Universi per Faciliorem Methodum ad Veram Praxim Sincere Redacti Compendium* (2 vols., Lutetiae Parisiorum, 1863), II, 63 (hereinafter cited *Juris Canonici Compendium)*.

2 Reiffenstuel, *Jus Canonicum Universum* (5 vols. in 7, Parisiis, 1864-1870), lib. V, tit. 39, n. 106 (hereinafter cited Reiffenstuel); Schmalzgrueber, *Jus Ecclesiasticum Universum* (5 vols. in 12, Romae, 1843-1845), lib. V, tit. 39, n. 216 (hereinafter cited Schmalzgrueber); Ferraris, *loc. cit.*

3 Canon 20 of this Council states: ". . . Si quis, ut diximus, ullum eorum, quocumque ordine consecratum, caesis vulneribus, vel quibuscumque iniuriis, angustiaverit, jubeat eum dominus episcopus per bannum a se impositum ante se venire, et advocet cognitorem et adjutorem comitem, et

this text as proof of the divine origin of the privilege of the canon, as Fagnanus (1598-1678) does, is anything but conclusive. The divine law as presented to us by the teaching of Christ forbids us to do wrong to our neighbor. In this sense every man has a right that his person and rights be respected by others. Furthermore, Fagnanus in a sense seems to contradict himself for in his *ex professo* written treatise on the privilege of the canon[4] he states that the privilege can easily be lost, since it derives only from custom. On the other hand, in the section in which he attempts to show tonsure to be of divine institution he uses the text of the above-mentioned Council to show that clerics in first tonsure enjoy the privilege by divine law.[5]

Rather, it should be argued that the words "*contra divinas . . . leges*" indicate, not that clerical immunity is formally of divine origin, but simply that the dignity of the clergy has its basis in the divine law. By reason of the superiority of the Church over the State the Church may grant to her clergy certain immunities, one of which is the privilege of the canon. It seems, therefore, more defensible to hold with Downs[6] that this privilege as one of the clerical immunities is in its juridical origin formally derived from ecclesiastical law.[7]

constringat protervum episcopus auctoritate canonica; ut eidem clerico, cui *contra divinas et humanas leges* contumelias ingressit, justam et debitam persolvat compositionem: et comite agente persolvat bannum regibus debitum." — Mansi, *Sacrorum Conciliorum Nova et Amplissima Collectio* (53 vols. in 60, Parisiis, 1901-1927), XVIII, 142-143. This collection will hereinafter be referred to as Mansi.

4 Fagnanus, *Commentaria in Quinque Libros Decretalium* (5 vols. in 3, Venetiis, 1709-1729), V, 335, n. 9.

5 Fagnanus, *op. cit.*, I, 424, nn. 81-82.

6 *The Concept of Clerical Immunity*, The Catholic University of America Canon Law Studies, n. 126 (Washington, D. C.: The Catholic University of America Press, 1941), p. 129.

7 It can be noted that the privilege of the canon is not referred to as an immunity in the Decretals of Gregory IX in the treatise on the excommunication of the Canon. However, the privilege of the canon is considered one of the personal immunities of clerics. Cf. Bernardus Papiensis, *Summa Decretalium* (ed. E. A. T. Laspeyres, Ratisbonae, 1860), Lib. III, tit. 36, § 3; Hostiensis, *Summa Aurea* (Venetiis, 1570), Lib. III, *de immunitate*

By way of conclusion from the foregoing it can be said almost apodictically that the privilege of the canon is not of divine origin. The overwhelming support of the authors substantiates this view. In ultimate analysis, however, it is of little practical import that this question be definitely solved. Pope Benedict XIV (1740-1758) goes so far as to call it superfluous to examine into the origin of clerical immunity.[8]

Article 2 — Protection of the Clergy under Roman Law

A. Justinian Code

One can readily see how the murder of a priest would as a crime come under the scope not only of ecclesiastical law but also of the civil law. Such an act exists as a matter of the mixed forum.[9] The Church is directly interested in matters pertaining to the administration of the Sacraments, the celebration of the sacred rites, and the maintenance of discipline in the Church. On the other hand, it is of direct concern to the State to see that peace and harmony prevail among its members. When the order that should prevail is disturbed, it is expected that the State should intervene. Special legislation in the Body of Civil Law in countries where Christianity had obtained legal recognition could quite naturally be expected for the case in which the crime involved a cleric as its victim.

Many authors state that in the early centuries the clergy were so esteemed by the people that the violation of the person of a cleric was a rare happening, and hence there was little or perhaps no need for specific legislation on this point.[10] Yet it is

ecclesiastica, p. 318, n. 15; Cappello, *Institutiones Iuris Publici Ecclesiastici* (2 vols., Augustae Taurinorum, 1907), I, 454.

8 *De Synodo Dioecesana* (2 vols., Romae, 1806), Lib. IX, tom. 1, cap. 9, n. 8.

9 Devoti, *Jus Canonicum Universum Publicum et Privatum* (3 vols., Romae, 1837), I, 268.

10 Wernz-Vidal, *Ius Canonicum* (7 vols. in 8, Romae: Universitas Gregoriana, 1928-1943), II *(Ius de Personis* [3. ed., 1943]), n. 74 (hereinafter this volume will be cited *Ius de Personis);* "Privilège" — *Dictionnaire Pratique des Connaissances Religieuses* (6 vols., Paris: Librairie Letouzey

difficult to imagine that the Church which had survived a persecution should in a short time become so respected by all that injuries against its clergy were practically unknown. The many martyrs among the clergy, not only during the time of persecution, but also during the centuries following, stand out as living testimony against this. Although the year 313 through the Edict of Milan brought an end to the persecution of Christians, crimes against the clergy must have been sufficiently frequent to merit judicial cognizance in later Roman Law.[11]

Crimes of this type were branded in the Civil Law as sacrilege, and were punished accordingly. It would be beyond the scope of this study to trace successively the various and manifold actions in which the Civil Law saw the presence of sacrilege, and consequently it will suffice to indicate how Roman Law proscribed and punished as a species of sacrilege any infringement of clerical dignity.

As early as the year 398, by a decree of Emperors Arcadius (395-408) and Honorius (395-423), anyone doing any injury to the priests and ministers of the Catholic Church was to receive capital sentence at the hands of the provincial authorities. The pertinent text reads: "If anyone should be guilty of the sacrilege of forcing his way into a Catholic church, or of doing any injury to the priests and ministers, to the service, or to the place itself, he shall be punished by the provincial authorities, so that the heads of the priests of the province and of the ministers of the Catholic Church may know that the culprit has received a capital sentence."[12]

In this text two points may be noted. First, such an injury was considered in Roman Law as a public crime. Secondly, the

et Ané, 1925-1928), II, 202; Gignac, *Compendium Juris Canonici* (2 vols., Quebec, 1901-1903), I, 121; Sebastianelli, *Praelectiones Juris Canonici*, I, *De Personis* (2. ed., Romae, 1905), p. 11.

11 Cf. Funk, *Manual of Church History*, translated from the German by P. Perciballi and edited by W. H. Kent (2 vols., London: Burns, Oates and Washbourne, Ltd., 1938), I, 115.

12 C. (I, 3) 10. This translation is taken from Scott, *The Civil Law* (17 vols. in 7, Cincinnati: The Central Trust Co., 1932), XII, 32.

crime itself called for capital punishment.[13] However, for the Romans capital punishment did not have the same connotation as it has in the Civil Codes of modern times. It was not always identified with the death penalty. Often it meant loss of both family and civic rights, or of the latter alone.[14] The law made the further provision that it was praiseworthy for all persons to prosecute as public crimes any atrocious injuries committed against priests or ministers of religion, since the perpetration of such misdeeds was deserving of condign punishment. No accusation was necessary. If delinquents armed themselves to resist civil authority in arresting them, the governors of the Provinces were to call for military assistance by public proclamation.[15]

B. Novels

Regarding these enactments a slight change was introduced in the Novels of Justinian. Under this later legislation anyone who entered a church during the celebration of the sacred rites and reviled the bishop, clerics or other ministers of the church was to be scourged and sent into exile. But if the culprit interrupted the service or forbade it to be conducted, he was to receive capital punishment for his crime. This latter rule was also to be observed with reference to the interruption of processions in which the bishop or clerics took part.[16] Another law ordered that those who attempted to annoy members of the clergy with insults, or abuse, or outrages, or with corporal injury, be punished with the greatest severity "after they had been deprived of their offices and patrimony." [17]

The importance of these regulations of Roman Law cannot be overestimated. Ecclesiastical legislation on this point was lacking, and in consequence the Church borrowed its norms and

13 Accursius ad C. (I, 3) 10 s. v. *si quis in hoc genus sacrilegii.*

14 Leage, *Roman Private Law* (2. ed. by C. H. Ziegler, London: Macmillan, 1942), p. 127.

15 Salvagio, *Antiquitatum Christianarum Institutiones* (6 vols., Venetiis, 1794), Tom. VI, lib. 4, pp. 93-94.

16 Nov. (123), 31.

17 C. (I, 3) 31.

directives from the Roman Law prescriptions.[18] The use of Roman Law as a supplementary source of ecclesiastical law was sanctioned by many of the Supreme Pontiffs. As late as the year 1917, although at the time Roman Law was no longer considered the supplementary source of law, Pope Benedict XV (1914-1922) in the Constitution *"Providentissima,"* by means of which he promulgated the Code of Canon Law, spoke of it as the "insigne veteris sapientiae monumentum." [19]

Article 3 — The Laws of the Carolingian Kings and of the "Barbaric Tribes"

It is not difficult for one to imagine the profound change the Gospel teaching effected in the lives of the people. Christianity introduced a more humane element into life in view of its opposition to slavery and gladiatorial combats. It encouraged charity to and relief of the unfortunate. These Christian influences changed the character of social life, and in turn brought on a change in the concept of man's juridical life. It is not necessary to discuss here the changes that came about with and through the foundation of the Church. But it should be noted that the influence of the Church was not confined to the early centuries. Also at a later time the elements of lenity and of forbearance which were incorporated in the Church's own system of law asserted themselves likewise in the Civil Law. This influence became noticeable particularly in the laws of the Carolingian Kingdom. The security of the State was no longer thought to be sufficiently protected solely by the sanction of death, but also through the infliction of salutary penances on the delinquents. The kings were most solicitous in being regarded as protectors of the Church. This solicitude found its plainest expression when

[18] Stutz, *Der Geist des Codex iuris canonici*, Kirchenrechtliche Abhandlungen hrsg. von Ulrich Stutz, 92. und 93. Heft (Stuttgart: Verlag von Ferdinand Enke, 1918), p. 188.

[19] *Acta Apostolicae Sedis, Commentarium Officiale* (Romae, 1909-1929; Civitate Vaticana, 1929 —), IX (1917), Pars II, 6. Hereafter cited *AAS*.

they enacted laws touching on Church matters, which laws became known as "Capitularies."[20]

In one of the Capitularies of Charlemagne a fine of 300 *solidi* was fixed as the penalty for the killing of a subdeacon; 400 for the killing of a deacon; 600 of a priest; 900 of a bishop; 400 of a monk.[21]

Slight variations are found in the laws of the different Germanic Tribes. Christianity did not everywhere spread in a peaceful manner. At times many killings and great violence characterized its spread among the barbarians. Yet it cannot be denied that these barbaric nations did recognize the dignity of the clerical state and accordingly took measures to protect the clergy. The laws of the *Ripuarii,* for example, indicated the sum of *solidi* to be paid as a penalty for the murder of the ministers of the Church. The amount of the penalty varied in accordance with the different status of the culprit, that is, with reference to his status as a slave, as a free person, as a cleric, etc. The Bavarians stipulated that the fine be paid in gold, if the culprit possessed it. If he did not possess gold he could be compelled to give in equivalent value the land or whatever else he had.[22]

Article 4 — The Penitentials

Thus far consideration has been given to the secular legislation which protected the clergy from corporal maltreatment.

20 Thomassinus, *Vetus et Nova Ecclesiae Disciplina circa Beneficia et Beneficiarios* (10 vols., Magontiaci, 1787), pars II, lib. I, c. LXXII, n. 1; DeClercq, *La Legislation Religieuse Franque de Clovis à Charlemagne* (507-814) (Louvain: Bureaux du Recueil Bibliothèque Franque de l'Université; Paris: Librairie du Recueil Sirey S. A., 1936), pp. v. and 171.

21 "Capitula Quae in Lege Salica Mittenda Sunt" — *Monumenta Germaniae Historica,* Legum Sectio II, *Capitularia Regum Francorum,* tom. I (ed. A. Boretius, Hannoverae, 1883), 113. This collection will hereinafter be abbreviated *MGH.*

22 N. V. of the *Lex Ripuaria* — *MGH,* Legum Sectio I, *Leges Nationum Germanicarum,* tom. V, pars I (ed. Rudolph Sohm, Hannoverae, 1883), pp. 66 and 67; C. 9 of the *Lex Baiuariorum* — *MGH,* Legum Sectio I, *Leges Nationum Germanicarum,* tom. V, pars II (ed. Ernest de Schwind, Hannoverae, 1926), pp. 280 and 281.

This period preceded the era in which the Church gave specific attention to this misdeed by legislation of her own. Before discussing the conciliar legislation one may duly note that, before the local Churches enacted specific ecclesiastical penalties against the perpetrators of corporal harm to the ministers of the Gospel, special cognizance was taken in the Penitential books with regard to those who were guilty of the murdering of priests. As has already been mentioned, this crime was considered as a qualified species of sacrilege.

The Penitentials represent a period of transition in the penitential discipline of the Church, i.e., a change from public to private penance.[23] This consequently led to an entire transformation in the practice of penance. The literature which intimately reflects this transition is that of the Penitentials.[24]

These books indicated for each kind of sin the expiation that was to be imposed on the penitent. Each of these books contained a list of the crimes and of the corresponding penalties. It was characteristic of these books that they reflected a decline or a mitigation in the ancient severity of the penitential canons. The Penitentials prescribed the penalties simply for the objective or material transgressions of the law.[25]

With proper allowance for the various territorial differences which characterized the Penitentials, it can be stated in general

23 Le Bras, "Penitentiels"—*Dictionnaire de Théologie Catholique* (14 vols., Paris: Librairie Letouzey et Ané, 1903-1939), XII, 1160; Cicognani, *Canon Law,* authorized English version by J. O'Hara and F. Brennan (2. revised ed., Philadelphia: Dolphin Press, 1935), p. 225; Tixeront, *History of Dogmas,* translated from 5. French ed. by H. L. B. (3 vols., London and St. Louis: Herder Book Co., Vol. III, 2. ed., 1926), III, 375; Duchesne, *Christian Worship: Its Origin and Evolution,* translated by M. L. McClure (New York and London, 1903), pp. 435-445.

24 Ludwig, "Geschichte des Sacrilegs nach den Quellen des katholischen Kirchenrects"—*Archiv für katholisches Kirchenrecht* (Innsbruck, 1857-1861; Mainz, 1862—), LXIX (1893), 190 (hereafter cited *AKKR).*

25 Müller, *Ethik und Recht in der Lehre von der Verantwortlichkeit* (Regensburg: Habbel, 1932), p. 44; Swoboda, *Ignorance in Relation to Imputability of Delicts,* The Catholic University of America Canon Law Studies, n. 143 (Washington, D. C.: The Catholic University of America Press, 1941), p. 21.

that the malicious bodily injury inflicted on clerics was listed in the Penitentials with its corresponding penance. The early Penitential books looked upon the assassination of clerics as qualified homicide, whereas the later books, notably that of Rhabanus Maurus (†856), regarded it as sacrilege.[26]

The penance specified in the *Poenitentiale Valicellanum II*, a Roman collection, for the murder of a priest or of a bishop was the handing over of the culprit to the court of the king. The murder of any other cleric or of a monk was to be given its judicial cognizance in the court of the bishop. Moreover the criminal agent had to lay aside any arms he bore, and was subjected to the performance of a ten years' penance, of which five years were to be spent in a fast on bread and water.[27]

The Penitential of Monte Cassino demanded that anyone who killed a bishop, a priest, a deacon, a cleric or a monk was to leave behind him everything that he possessed and thereafter was to dedicate himself to the service of God.[28]

On the other hand, according to the Penitential of Arundel persons who were guilty of the crime of killing a deacon or a monk were to perform a ten years' penance. This same Penitential specified nine years of penance for the murder of a subdeacon.[29]

Among the Anglo-Saxon Penitentials that which is attributed to Theodore of Canterbury (†690) is worthy of mention, for in it the murder of a priest is treated as qualified homicide, and the person who slew a monk or a cleric was obliged to lay aside his arms and serve God, or as an alternative was to perform a seven years' penance. This crime was adjudicated in the court of the bishop. But it was reserved for the king to pass judgment on the crime of one who slew a bishop or a priest.[30]

From these few excerpts collected from various Penitentials

26 *AKKR, loc. cit.;* Schmitz, *Die Bussbücher und die Bussdisciplin der Kirche* (Mainz, 1883), pp. 355-737.

27 Schmitz, *op. cit.*, p. 355.

28 Schmitz, *op. cit.*, p. 402.

29 Schmitz, *op. cit.*, p. 437.

30 McNeill-Gamer, *Medieval Handbooks of Penance*, a translation of the

representative of the disciplinary practice current in different countries scarcely any manifestation of development is to be found in the penances and penal sanctions imposed for the murder of priests or of clerics. It seems, too, that the Penitentials were concerned solely with the question of the murdering of the clergy, and prescinded entirely from any and all consideration of real injury in which death did not follow. Hence it cannot be said that there is any direct reference in the Penitentials to the privilege of the canon. The above presented details, however, were introduced simply for the purpose of indicating that the earlier Penitentials viewed the murder of priests as qualified homicide and the later Penitentials viewed it as a sacrilege. From this one can conclude that the dignity of the priesthood was recognized as calling for a special respect, and that in consequence the wilful taking of the life of a priest was regarded as a special kind of crime. The privilege of the canon was the outgrowth of the respect which the laity manifested for the clergy.

principal *libri poenitentiales* and selections from related documents (New York: Columbia University Press, 1938), p. 187. This work is n. XXIX of the Series: *Records of Civilization, Sources and Studies,* edited under the auspices of the Department of History, Columbia University.

CHAPTER II

PARTICULAR ECCLESIASTICAL LEGISLATION

Article 1 — The Ninth Century

Just as secular rulers, princes and kings are especially protected by the Civil Law from bodily harm, so also the royal dignity of the priesthood is protected in all priests. Priests are *personae sacrosanctae.* Any harm or real injury inflicted on them is harm or injury perpetrated against something sacred, and therefore stands branded as sacrilegious. In the early centuries of the Church's history, it has been noted, harm or injury inflicted on clergymen was not considered as a crime specifically distinct from sacrilege. Accordingly it drew upon itself the specific penalty which was imposed for sacrilege, whether by the law of the Church, or by the statutes of the civil authority. Another reason which may be adduced in possible explanation for the meagerness of legislation regarding a crime which certainly must have occurred at some time or other is that the Church was preoccupied in her growth and extension with the combating of the early heresies.

An examination of the sources reveals that before the ninth century there was no specific mention in law regarding any penalty to be imposed in consequence of a real injury inflicted on the clergy. Moreover, the contention that legal preoccupation with this question arose in the ninth century seems to be corroborated by the fact that legislation on this point is readily recognized as dovetailing with the purpose of the pseudo-Isidorian compilers. Their purpose was to fortify and strengthen the position and rights of the bishops and to safeguard the administration of ecclesiastical property under them. This could be accomplished best if the person of the bishop was honored as inviolable.

In the year 821 a council was held at the village of Diedenhofen (Thionville) at which 32 bishops were present in order to take action against murderers and the malicious strikers of clerics.[1] Attacks against clerics had increased to such an extent that the bishops petitioned Louis the Pious (814-840): first, that the fines against the culprits be increased; secondly, that these fines be given to the bishops; and thirdly, that the guilty ones moreover be subjected to the ecclesiastical penalties determined in the council. Only four canons were drawn up in this council. They treated respectively of the canonical penalty established for calumniating, injuring or maiming subdeacons, deacons, priests and bishops. The canons mention the number of years of penance to be performed and the amount of the fine to be imposed. Louis the Pious in a decree heeded the request of the bishops by increasing the fine, which thereafter was to be given to the bishop or to his church. Also a public penance was to be performed. In consequence of the Emperor's decree the rule was: "Poenitentia canonica poeniteat. Juxta id, quod canones praecipiunt, poeniteat. Ut synodus dijudicaverit, poeniteat."[2]

In accordance with the wishes of King Louis II, the German (843-876), Rhabanus Maurus, Archbishop of Mainz, held a provincial council in the city of Mainz in the year 847. Specific mention was made in this council of the penalty inflicted for the murdering of a priest.[3] The guilty person was to perform a twelve years' penance according to the tenor of the canons already in force. A free man who denied his guilt was called on to swear to that denial along with 72 compurgators. A slave had to vindicate himself in trial by means of an ordeal. A convicted man was deprived of the right to bear arms for the rest of his days and he sacrificed also the prospect of marriage. A crime of this kind demanded satisfaction in the form of public penance.[4]

1 Hefele-Leclercq, *Histoire des Conciles* (10 vols. in 19, Paris: Librairie Letouzey et Ané, 1907-1938), IV, 32-35; Thomassinus, *Vetus et Nova Ecclesiae Disciplina,* Pars II, lib. I, c. LXXII, n. 2; Mansi, XIV, 390.

2 Thomassinus, *loc. cit.*

3 Can. 24—C. 24, C. XVII, q. 4; Mansi, XIV, 910; Hefele-Leclercq, *op. cit.*, IV, 134.

4 "Qui presbiterum occiderit, duodecim annorum ei poenitentia secundum canones imponatur; aut si negaverit, si liber est, cum septuaginta duobus iuret: si autem servus, super duodecim vomeres ferventes se expurget.

In the year 862 an important change in the legislation hitherto prevailing was introduced. Pope Nicholas I (858-867) was the reigning Pope. Under his guidance a Synod of many bishops was held at Rome. Because of the abuses which had been heaped upon the bishops, especially in Germany, the Pope established for the first time an excommunication against those who presumed to strike, to beat or to kill a bishop. The words of the Council read: "De his autem qui Episcopum percutere, verberare, aut caedere praesumpserint, ut anathematis subiaceant periculo, sancimus, et inviolabili promulgatione statuimus."[5] It is noteworthy that the liability of the penalty was incurred only by those who violated the person of a bishop.

Interesting legislation was enacted by the Council of Worms in the year 868. Canon 25 of this Council stated that any secular person convicted of attempting to molest a cleric was to be deprived of entrance into the church and at the same time lost his right to communion with his fellow Catholics. Canon 26 indicated the penance to be performed by the one who murdered a priest. The delinquent was not allowed to eat meat or to drink wine. Fasting was prescribed until Vespers every day except Sundays and Holy Days. The use of a vehicle of any description was forbidden for ten years, and consequently all journeys had to be made on foot. The excommunication continued for a period of five years.[6]

By the end of the ninth century it was a well established fact in Italy that bodily injury wrought against clerics was counted a sacrilege. This appears from a council held at Ravenna in the year 877 under Pope John VIII (872-882).[7]

Convictus vero noxae usque ad ultimum vitae tempus militiae cingulo careat, et absque spe coniugii maneat."

5 Caput XII — Mansi, XV, 660. Sägmüller *(Lehrbuch des katholischen Kirchenrechts* [2 vols., Freiburg im Breisgau, 1900-1904], I, 186) and Wernz-Vidal *(Ius de Personis,* n. 74) stated that the penalty enacted in this fourteenth canon was incurred *ipso facto.* The wording of the canon itself, however, seems to militate against this interpretation.

6 Mansi, XV, 874.

7 Can. 5 — C. 21, C. XVII, q. 4; Mansi, XVII, 338. This first appearance of the concept of sacrilege may be considered as an extension of the

At the close of the ninth century (895), Emperor Arnulphus (887-899) assembled the bishops of Germany in a Council at Tribur to reform the morals and status of both clergy and laity. Abuses indulged in by the laity against the clergy were discussed. The Council, however, seems to have accepted the provisions already prevailing in Germany regarding the infliction of penalties for the perpetrated death and injury to clerics. As has already been indicated, the usual penalty for such a crime was the pecuniary compensation or wergild.[8] Accepting this as the penalty, the Council simply commanded that the injured priest was to receive the entire compensation. If death had followed the injury, then there was a division of the wergild into three parts, one of which was to go to the church of the deceased, one to his bishop, and one to his parents.[9]

Up to this point mention has been made of the local conciliar regulations which had an immediate bearing on the topic under discussion. Two Italian Councils were considered, namely, those of Rome and Ravenna; three German Councils, Mainz, Worms and Tribur; and one Frankish, Thionville. Attention should be called to the fact that the German conciliar statutes were profoundly influenced by the provisions of the Germanic law. On the other hand, the Italian Councils were more directly concerned with strictly ecclesiastical penalties. Special emphasis has been put on the ninth century law, since this was the first

decree of Emperors Arcadius and Honorius referred to above. This decree restricted the sacrilege to the violation of a sacred place or to the violation of the person of a priest or other minister in a sacred place. The Roman law took no cognizance of an injury perpetrated outside a sacred place. In ecclesiastical law the sacrilege was extended to the violation of the person of a cleric even outside a sacred place.

8 The Teutonic Codes were based on the right of private war and private vengeance. The wergild, then, in both Anglo-Saxon and Germanic law, was the value set upon a man's life; it was a fixed price to be paid by the kindred of a manslayer to the slain person as compensation to avoid the blood feud. There was a fixed scale of values which varied from that of the churl to that of the king. Originally the acceptance of the wergild by the kindred of the person killed was optional. Later it became compulsory.

9 Canon IV — Mansi, XVIIa, 135.

legislation in the Church wherein the crime under discussion was given consideration apart from the general regulations regarding sacrilege.

Chronologically a discussion of the regulations adopted during the tenth century would be in order. But for the most part the legislation of the preceding century prevailed. Before an approach will be made to the study of the universal legislation, consideration will be given to a few salient factors which in the eleventh century to some extent influenced the Holy See to act.

Article 2 — The Eleventh Century

A. *Treuga Dei*

The Church had struggled unsuccessfully during the preceding centuries in her attempt to restrain the unscrupulous dukes and barons from their mutual feuds. She was especially interested in having protection for the unarmed clergyman, but it seems that the times were not yet ripe for the inauguration of an era of peace. The Church at first attempted to stop these feuds completely, but failing in this she endeavored to limit them as much as possible. This limitation of the right of perpetual warfare was reduced to writing, and sanctioned by an oath. After its confirmation by decrees of the Councils it was known as the "Truce of God."[10] This term was often used synonymously with the term "Peace of God." A distinction, however, should be made between the two. The phrase "Peace of God," older in origin, connoted the aim of effecting the absolute cessation of feudal hostilities on all days, whereas the

10 Ferraris, *Bibliotheca*, VII, 518; sub v. "treuga"; Hefele-Leclercq, *Histoire des Conciles*, IV, 698; Wernz-Vidal, *Ius de Personis*, n. 74; "Truce of God" — *Catholic Encyclopedia* (15 vols., Index, and 2 Supplements, New York, 1907-1922), XV, 68; Mourret, *A History of the Catholic Church*, translated by Newton Thompson (6 vols., St. Louis and London: Herder Book Co., 1930-1946), IV, 212; Pollock-Maitland, *History of English Law before the Time of Edward I* (2. ed., 2 vols., Cambridge, 1899), I, 75; Albers, *Manuel d'Histoire Ecclésiastique*, adaption de la seconde Édition Hollandaise par René Hedde (2 vols., Paris: Gabalda, 1923), I, 394. The last mentioned author refers the reader to additional literature on this subject.

"Truce of God" connoted the stipulation of intervals, known in Civil Law as *"induciae,"* when warfare was to cease.

The "truce" may be defined as a certain security granted to persons or places, even though the war had not ended, or the disagreement itself had not been settled. Two types of "truces" were known, the conventional and the canonical.[11] The former was a spontaneous free-will agreement between the contesting parties. The canonical truce was that constituted by the canon or by law. By the *"treuga Dei"* a suspension of warfare prevailed from Wednesday evening till Monday morning in every week from the beginning of Advent to the Octave of the Epiphany, and from the beginning of Lent until the Octave of Pentecost. This suspension of warfare was in effect also on the feast of the Holy Cross, on the three great feasts of the Virgin Mary, on the feasts of the twelve Apostles and of a few other saints. A contumacious violation after a threefold warning was punished with excommunication.[12]

It was by means of the *"treuga Dei"* that the Church exercised her authority for the protection of her clergy against personal violence during the early eleventh century. But even these measures proved ineffectual, and hence more stringent regulations became necessary. These measures came from a Council held at the Lateran in the year 1097.[13] In this Council, Urban II, the reigning Pontiff, inflicted a major excommunication on anyone who laid violent hands on a cleric or a monk. Except in the case

11 *Glossa Ordinaria,* ad c. 1, X, *de treuga et pace,* I, 34, s. v. "treuga."

12 Cf. Synodale Decretum de Pace apud Cadomum, 1042 — Mansi, XIX, 598.

13 That Urban II (1088-1099) held this Council in January, 1097, is known only from his letters. "De statu nostro nobiscum Deo gratias age, usque ad Urbem cum com. M. pacifice venimus, Urbem honestissime cum procedentium stipatione frequentissima introivimus, Urbem ipsam maiori iam ex parte habemus; Synodum Laterani solemniter celebravimus . . ." — Jaffé, *Regesta Pontificum ab condita Ecclesia ad annum post Christum natum MCXCVIII* (2. ed. cura Wattenbach, Kaltenbrunner, Ewald, Loewenfeld, 2 vols. in 1, Lipsiae, 1885-1888), n. 5678; Hefele-Leclercq, *Histoire des Conciles,* V, 453. Hereafter the work of Jaffé will be referred to simply as Jaffé.

of danger of death, absolution from the incurred excommunication was reserved to the Holy See.[14]

B. The Lay Investiture Struggle

The problem of feudal warfare was not the only problem the Church had to face in the eleventh century. An issue with even deeper roots and more far-reaching effects was the lay investiture controversy. Lay investiture was a great evil, for it was the root of simony. The core of this controversy centered in Germany.

The manner in which high ecclesiastical dignities were conferred, that is, in accordance with the institutions of the preceding period, placed the Church in too great dependence on the State. The king for his part regarded bishoprics as being within his power to bestow. He allowed no bishop to exercise his functions until he was invested by the king with ring and staff. To the Church the use of these symbols betokened the conferring by the king of spiritual functions. It was Pope Gregory VII (1073-1085) who took most energetic measures to put an end to this abuse. But his attempt brought a violent reaction from the secular power, especially from Henry IV of Germany (1056-1106).

Lay investiture could not at once be wholly abolished, for the acknowledged factor of legal prescription had *prima facie* given it a title to some consideration. Henry IV was unwilling to yield. His refusal to meet the demands of the Pope occasioned dire consequences. In fact it led to war, as a result of which many real injuries were inflicted on the clergy. Those who rallied to the support of the Pontiff suffered many violences at the hands of those who rallied to the side of the Emperor. The Emperor and his adherents did not limit their atrocities to priests, but even violated the person of the Pope himself.

On Christmas eve in the year 1075 Pope Gregory VII was

[14] Hefele-Leclercq reproduce canon 6 of this Council thus: "Quiconque frappera violemment un clerc ou un moine sera puni d'anathème, et, sauf le cas de mort, ne pourra être absous que par le siège apostolique." — *Histoire des Conciles*, V, 455. The text of this Council is not reproduced in the collections of the Councils.

severely struck and then seized in the Church of St. Mary Major, thereupon to be forcefully brought to the house of the Cencius family, where he was imprisoned in a tower near the Pantheon. But he was almost immediately rescued from his captivity by an immense and tumultuous throng. The Pope was then accompanied by the crowd back to the Church of St. Mary Major on Christmas morning.

These few points concerning the lay investiture struggle have been introduced for the sake of showing that assaults of a most shocking nature were inflicted on the clergy. If even the sacred dignity of the Pope's person was not respected in this great struggle, then it can be assumed *a fortiori* that the dignity of the lesser clergymen was subjected to at least equal outrage.[15]

Article 3 — Early Twelfth Century Councils

The early twelfth century brought very trying times to the Church, for both heresy and schism existed as threatening dangers. The most active agitator of the times was the ultimately unsuccessful political reformer, Arnold of Brescia (1100-1155). He caused great commotion by his unjustified attack on the clergy and by his stubborn attempts to turn the laity against the clergy.[16]

To combat the errors which gave rise to this kind of opposition Innocent II (1130-1143) convoked a council at Clermont in the year 1130. At this Council was issued the canon which later was to be incorporated almost in its entirety in the universal law of the Church: "Item placuit ut si quis, suadente diabolo, huius

[15] The literature on this controversy is abundant. The reader is referred to the following literature, and also to the books and articles there listed: Brooke, "Gregory VII and the First Contest between Empire and Papacy"—*The Cambridge Medieval History* (8 vols., New York: Macmillan Co., 1911-1936, Vol. V, edited by J. R. Tanner, C. W. Privité-Orton and Z. N. Brooke), V, 58-77; Poulet, *A History of the Catholic Church,* authorized translation and adaptation from the fourth French edition by Sidney Raemers (2 vols., St. Louis and London: Herder, 1941-1945), I, 440-443; Albers, *Manuel D'Histoire Ecclésiastique,* I, 423.

[16] Phillips, *Kirchenrecht* (7 vols., Regensburg, 1845-1872, Vol. VIII, 1,

sacrilegii reatum incurrerit, quo in clericos vel monachos manus iniecerit, anathemati subjaceat. Quod qui fecerit, excommunicetur."[17]

In the following year the same provision was adopted at the Council of Rheims, but this Council added the further obligation of journeying to Rome for absolution from this excommunication.[18]

by F. Vering, Regensburg, 1889), I, 660; Schaff, *History of the Christian* Church (7 vols., Vol. V by David S. Schaff, New York, 1907), V, 97.

17 Canon 10 — Mansi, XXI, 439. Cf. Hinschius, *Das Kirchenrecht der Katholiken und Protestanten in Deutschland* (6 vols., Berlin, 1869-1897), I, 118. Hereinafter cited *Das Kirchenrecht.*

18 Canon 13: ". . . Et nullus episcoporum illud [i. e., anathema] praesumat absolvere, donec apostolico conspectui praesentetur, et eius mandatum suscipiat." — Mansi, XXI, 461. This same canon was adopted by the Council of Pisa in 1135. — Mansi, XXI, 490.

CHAPTER III

LEGISLATION IN THE *CORPUS IURIS CANONICI*

Article 1 — The II General Council of the Lateran (1139)

Before the year 1139 the excommunication enacted against those who inflicted real (bodily) injury on clerics was decreed solely in particular councils, and therefore did not exist with the force of universal law. The respect once fostered by the laity for the clergy had waned, and the laity became more and more guilty of excesses against the clergy. These excesses were in large measure instigated by obstreperous heretics. The prevailing discipline had made it impossible for an accusation to be made against a cleric, and as a consequence the laity took it upon themselves to punish any misdemeanors of which they thought the clergy guilty.[1]

The legislation passed by the II General Council of the Lateran (1139) came as a consequence of the heresy and schism which threatened the Church at the time. At that time Arnold of Brescia directed his attacks against the clergy. His violence sprang from his heretical teaching that any cleric who held property, any bishop who held crown revenues, or any monk who had any possession whatever, could not be saved.[2] The attacks of these heretical agitators upon ecclesiastics and monks aroused popular passion to such an extent that it became necessary to take more stringent measures for the protection of their person. These circumstances, then, led to the convocation of the II General Council of the Lateran under Innocent II.[3]

The Fathers of the Council in an effort to restrain these antagonists extended to the Church universally what had pre-

1 "Privilège" — *Dictionnaire Pratique des Connaissances Religieuses,* II, 202; Gignac, *Compendium Juris Canonici,* I *(De Personis),* 11.

2 Zitelli-Natali, *Epitome Historico-Canonica Conciliorum Generalium* (Romae, 1881), p. 143; Funk, *Manual of Church History,* I, 388.

3 Mosheim, *An Ecclesiastical History, Ancient and Modern,* translated from the Latin by Archibald Maclaine (6 vols., London, 1825), III, 119.

viously existed only as particular law. The privilege of the canon is contained in the famous fifteenth Canon of this Council and reads as follows:

> Item placuit, ut si quis suadente diabolo huius sacrilegii reatum incurrit, quod in clericum vel monachum violentas manus injecerit, anathematis vinculo subjaceat: et nullus episcoporum illum praesumat absolvere, nisi mortis urgente periculo: donec apostolico conspectui praesentetur, et eius mandatum suscipiat. Praecipimus etiam, ut in eos, qui ad ecclesiam vel coemeterium confugerint, nullus omnino manum mittere audeat. Quod si fecerit, excommunicetur.[4]

Article 2 — The Canon in the Decree of Gratian

The II General Council of the Lateran was held in the year 1139. In that year or shortly thereafter appeared the Decree of Gratian.[5] For that reason one is not to look to Gratian for much more than a terse statement regarding the canon which enacted the excommunication. In the second part of the *Decretum,* where Gratian considers the question of personal sacrilege, there are listed ten canons, three of which are *Paleae,* and therefore not originally part of the *Decretum.*[6] In these canons Gratian explained the concept of sacrilege according to the ecclesiastical sources.[7] However, he also made mention of the notion as it was

4 Mansi, XXI, 530. Schroeder *(Disciplinary Decrees of the General Councils,* Text, Translation, and Commentary [London-St. Louis: Herder Book Co., 1937], pp. 204-205) offers the following translation of this canon: "If anyone at the instigation of the devil incurs the guilt of this sacrilege, namely, that he has laid violent hands on a cleric or monk, he shall be anathematized and no bishop shall dare absolve him, except *mortis urgente periculo,* till he be presented to the Apostolic See and receive its mandate. We command also that no one shall dare lay hands on those who have taken refuge in a church or cemetery. Anyone doing this, let him be excommunicated."

5 Kuttner, "The Father of the Science of Canon Law," — *The Jurist* (Published by the School of Canon Law: The Catholic University of America, Washington, D. C., 1941 —), I (1941), 3, n. 2; Plöchl, *Das Eherecht des Magisters Gratianus* (Leipzig und Wien: Franz Deuticke, 1935), p. 14.

6 C. 12, 21, 22, 23, 27, 28, 29, C. XVII, q. 4. Under the same *Causa* and *Questio* the following are *Paleae:* c. 24, 25, 26.

7 *Dictum* ad c. 29, C. XVII, q. 4.

contained in Roman Law.[8] An analysis of the canons as contained in Gratian indicates that the law prevailing at that time in punishment for the malicious striking of clerics could be summed up in a very concise formula. The impious bodily assault and attack on clerics was treated as a sacrilege, which was punished by fine and excommunication. The fine was to be paid to those who had suffered from the sacrilegious action.[9]

A. *Canons on Personal Sacrilege Reproduced by Gratian*[10]

In one of his *Dicta* Gratian indicated that sacrilege was present "quoties qui sacrum violat, vel auferendo sacrum de sacro, vel sacrum de non sacro, vel non sacrum de sacro. Dicitur etiam sacrilegium committere qui violentas et impias manus in clericum iniecerit." [11]

Of the seven canons which Gratian listed as bearing on the privilege of the canon, two make mention that the violent bodily attack upon a cleric constitutes a sacrilege.[12] Sacrilege was considered as a more heinous sin than fornication; the latter was a trespass on the dignity of man, but the former was an encroachment on the very sphere of God.

The remaining five canons treat of the penalties incurred by the one who was guilty of personal sacrilege. Among these five it is canon 29 that repeats the legislation of the II Lateran Council enacted against malicious strikers of clerics. Two other canons in this section mention excommunication as a vindicative penalty when the guilty person remained contumacious.[13] The fines as imposed by Charlemagne (†814) on those who killed a priest, a deacon, a subdeacon or a monk were incorporated as law in the twenty-seventh canon.[14] The last canon pertaining to this

8 *Dictum* ad c. 29, C. XVII, q. 4.

9 Ludwig, "Geschichte des Sacrilegs" — *AKKR*, LXIX (1893), 226-228.

10 All of these canons can be found in C. XVII, q. 4.

11 *Dictum* ad c. 21, C. XVII, q. 4.

12 C. 12, 21, C. XVII, q. 4.

13 C. 22, 23, C. XVII, q. 4.

14 This has been treated above in the article dealing with the laws of the Carolingian Kings and the "Barbaric Tribes."

group makes mention of the public penance that was to be performed by those who had been guilty of personal sacrilege.

B. The PALEAE Treating of Personal Sacrilege

The authors of the *Paleae* incorporated three canons from earlier conciliar statutes. Canon 24 contains the legislation of the Council of Mainz (847), which has already been discussed. Canons 25 and 26 contain purported enactments of the Council of Tribur (895).[15] Both of these canons speak of the fine imposed on violators of the person of the cleric. Mention is made of the persons to whom the fine is to be paid.

Article 3 — The Nature of the Penalty

In crystal-clear words the Lateran Council indicated that the penalty determined for the sacrilegious mistreatment of clerics was excommunication. What was not so clear was whether the penalty was of a *latae sententiae* or a *ferendae sententiae* character in the original intention of the legislator. Indeed, with Phillips (1804-1872)[16] it can be stated that for all practical purpose the theoretical doubt was of no import, since it was a well established fact that by 1157-1159 the enacted excommunication was acknowledged as a *latae sententiae* penalty.[17]

Hinschius (1835-1898), in his treatment concerning the position of the clergy, stated: "The penalty for the above mentioned action (the malicious striking of clerics) is a major excommunication, and according to the original meaning of the canon should stand as a *ferendae sententiae* excommunication. But before the end of the twelfth century the universal legislation as well as the teaching and practice indicated it to be a *latae sententiae* penalty."[18] As authority for his statement he referred the reader to

15 Friedberg in his critical edition of the *Decretum Gratiani* indicates in a footnote that the text of these canons is not traceable in that Council.

16 *Kirchenrecht*, I, 666.

17 Rufinus († ca. 1190), who wrote at that time, referred to the excommunication as being incurred *ipso iure*. — *Summa Decretorum* (ed. H. Singer, Paderborn, 1902), p. 273.

18 *Kirchenrecht*, I, 121.

a brochure written by Hüffer (1830-1905), the text of which appeared in Volume III of the *Archiv für katholisches Kirchenrecht.*[19] Hüffer argued that in view of the gravity of the crime of laying violent hands on a cleric an extraordinary penalty was postulated, but an excommunication *ferendae sententiae* was severe enough in view of the fact that the absolution from the penalty was reserved to the Holy See. He further argued that the text of the universal law was taken from the enactments of the Council of Clermont (1130), whose legislation was repeated as late as one year before the II Lateran Council by the Council of London (1138). In this latter Council the excommunication was levied only after a threefold warning, and hence Hüffer was unwilling to admit that one year later the excommunication had assumed the character of a *latae sententiae* penalty.[20]

Berardi (1719-1768) held the same opinion. He maintained that in examining the canon of the II Lateran Council one could not immediately and easily conclude that the canon was to be understood as enacting a *latae sententiae* penalty. He argued that the phrase *"anathematis vinculo subiaceat"* had the same meaning as *"sit anathematizatus"* or *"sit ab ecclesiastica communione sequestratus,"* and indicated accordingly that a pronouncement of sentence had to intervene. Further, he argued that this penalty was enacted at a time when *latae sententiae* penalties were unheard of, and when an admonition had of necessity to precede the incurring of any penalty.[21]

While these arguments admittedly seem to offer a strong support for the view that the fifteenth canon of the II Lateran Council was enacted as a *ferendae sententiae* penalty, nevertheless a more careful analysis will indicate that the view is untenable.

First, it is to be noted that Rufinus († ca. 1190), who was a

19 Pp. 155-169.

20 Canon 10 of the Council of London stated: "Si quis clericum vel monachum vel sanctimonialem vel quamlibet ecclesiasticam personam occiderit, incarceraverit vel nefarias ei manus intulerit, nisi tertio submonitus satisfecerit, anathemate feriatur." — Mansi, XXI, 512.

21 Berardi, *Gratiani Canones Genuini ab Apocryphis Discreti* (2. ed. Veneta, 3 vols. in 4, Venetiis, 1783), Pars II, tom. 2, c. ult., p. 393.

disciple of Gratian († ca. 1150) and who wrote his treatise less than twenty years (1157-1159) after the II Lateran Council, espoused the *latae sententiae* interpretation of the canon. If there had been any question in the mind of Gratian or of the canonists of the time concerning the nature of this penalty, then one could surely look for some mention of this from Rufinus.

Secondly, the form of the wording employed in the Council of London does not militate against the *latae sententiae* effect in the legislation of the subsequent general council. Because of the frequency of violent acts against the clergy the Church could well deem it necessary to draft severer penalties in dealing with such delinquents. Furthermore, a comparison of the text of the II Lateran Council with the texts of the Council of Clermont and of London shows that the wording of the universal law was influenced directly only by the former of these councils. Since many of the territories where violences of this sort were common had already adopted the policy of inflicting excommunication for such acts, and since the commission of the crime did not cease but rather increased, so that more effective legislation from Rome itself became necessary, it seems that the Church had in mind the enactment of a penalty which became operative with the very commission of the misdeed. Intervention on the part of Rome would have been unnecessary, for the bishops in many territories had already exercised their power of inflicting excommunication for such a crime.

Thirdly, there is no reason to suppose that this legislation first existed as implying the incurring of a penalty only upon a previous judicial sentence, and only later through usage and doctrine came to be regarded as a *latae sententiae* penalty. Such a conclusion seems unjustified, for if there had been a change in policy, one would look to Rome for some mention of it.

Fourthly, the opinion that the enacted excommunication existed from the beginning as a *latae sententiae* penalty has the overwhelming support of authority. The Popes, the Glossators, and practically all the writers accepted this concept of the penalty without any doubt or hesitation.[22]

22 That the *Glossa* in the Roman edition of 1582 calls the canon a

Fifthly, the argument adduced by Berardi that the legislation came at a time when *latae sententiae* penalties were not in vogue is not a conclusive one. It is in effect a striking example of the *petitio principii.* But it does appear defensible to regard this particular excommunication as a penalty which was the first of its type, that is, a penalty which was incurred in direct and inseparable connection with the perpetration of a physical assault and attack on a cleric or a monk. Later ages saw the establishment of many penalties of this type.

Article 4 — The Canon in the Decretals

The work of Gratian had constituted a basic source for the commentary offered by the Glossators. Likewise, even before the time of the later Decretalists, there developed in richer detail an understanding in respect of the privilege of the canon in view of the Decretal legislation which, in the course of the nine and a half decades that elapsed between the appearance of Gratian's work and the official publication of the Decretals of Gregory IX, had emanated from the Roman Pontiffs by way of further interpretation. The canon of the II Lateran Council constituted a cynosure for papal legislation during the next one hundred years. All of this papal legislation served to amplify in greater detail the legislation already enacted. For this reason, then, a more detailed study of the law as it is found in the Decretals seems fully apropos.[23]

ferendae sententiae penalty has been acknowledged as a printing error. At the time of the writing of the *Glossa* (1215) the penalty was accepted as a *latae sententiae* penalty. — Hinschius, *Das Kirchenrecht,* I, 121, n. 8; Phillips, *Kirchenrecht,* I, p. 666, n. 46. Even Hüffer *(loc. cit.)*, who supported the opinion that the fifteenth canon of the II General Council of the Lateran enacted a *ferendae sententiae* penalty, admitted that no argument could be drawn from the fact that the *Glossa* stated that this penalty was not a *latae sententiae* penalty.

23 Some of the Decretal enactments with regard to the privilege of the canon will not be discussed at this point, but will be discussed more fully in the canonical commentary.

ARTICLE 5 — PERSONS ENJOYING THE PRIVILEGE

The canon which enacted the excommunication threatened those who maliciously inflicted a real (bodily) injury on a "cleric" or on a "monk." Since there was question of a penalty one might be led to conclude that the canon was to receive a strict interpretation. But, on the other hand, one sees in the law a privilege granted by the legislator to those in the service of the Lord. Hence, according to a very ancient principle of law, later incorporated in the *Regulae Juris* of Boniface VIII, a broad interpretation was in order: "Odia restringi, et favores convenit ampliari." [24]

The protection of this canon was enjoyed, then, by all those who had received the first tonsure, and by all those who were constituted in orders, whether major or minor.[25] And if clerics in first tonsure and minor orders, and also priests were protected, then *a fortiori* the bishops, the cardinals, and the Pope were included in the same protection. However, if a cleric did not wear the tonsure, or if he laid aside his clerical garb, then he lost the protecting influence of this canon upon a threefold unheeded warning.[26]

The entire category of those who took vows in a religious community, whether those who pledged them were men or women, came under the generic name of "monk." [27] This privilege was later extended by Pope Boniface VIII (1294-1303) to the novices.[28]

[24] Reg. 15, R. J., in VI°.

[25] "Numquid qui tales percutiunt incidunt in canonem latae sententiae? Dico quod sic, quia clerici sunt et quicumque clericum percutit excommunicatus est." — *Glossa Ordinaria* ad c. 11, X, *de aetate et qualitate et ordine praeficiendorum,* I, 14, s. v. "ordo confertur."

[26] C. 45, X, *de sententia excommunicationis,* V, 39; Potthast, *Regesta Pontificum Romanorum inde ab anno post Christum natum MCXCVIII ad MCCCIV* (2 vols., Berolini, 1874-1875), n. 4641.

[27] C. 33, X, *de sententia excommunicationis,* V, 39. In the earlier days of the Church women of religious communities were customarily included even under the name of clerics. Cf. c. 7, C. XII, q. 1.

[28] C. 21, *de sententia excommunicationis, suspensionis et interdicti,* V, 11, in VI°.

Article 6 — Persons Excluded from the Penalty

Most of the chapters contained in the thirty-ninth title of the last book of the Gregorian Decretals deal with the excommunication incurred through a violation of the privilege of the canon. In these chapters specific examples are given which indicate which injurious actions against clerics did not entail the incurring of the enacted censure. According to the fifteenth canon of the II General Council of the Lateran the censure of excommunication enacted against the *percussores clericorum* was not incurred unless the inflicted violence was prompted *"suadente diabolo."* This legislation was clarified in the Decretal law by the enunciation of principles, and especially by the indication of specific examples.

The words used by the Council of the Lateran indicate that knowledge of the wrongfulness of the act and also the personal intention to perpetrate it were postulated on the part of the wrong-doer. The act had to be of a gravely injurious character both materially and formally.[29] This did not imply that the person who inflicted the injury had to be motivated by a hatred against his contemplated clerical victim. The delinquent's act entailed excommunication when it was committed with a malicious intention. Hence the persons who by law were excused from incurring the excommunication had to be presumed to act without a malicious intention.[30] Thus a father or a superior who chastised a young cleric did not do so with the intention of inflicting a real injury on him.[31] Also a man who rose up in self-defense against an attacking cleric was presumed not to have any malicious intention of striking the cleric;[32] it was simply assumed that he sought a means of self-protection which he recognized as warranted by the very first law of nature.[33]

29 Cf. Hostiensis, *Summa Aurea*, lib. V, *de sententia excommunicationis*, n. 10.

30 Cf. *infra*, pp. 98-104.

31 C. 1, 10, 54, X, *de sententia excommunicationis*, V, 39. Cf. Jaffé, n. 8987.

32 C. 3, X, *de sententia excommunicationis*, V, 39.

33 The Decretalists developed this doctrine chiefly by comparing the

ARTICLE 7 — PERSONS LIABLE TO THE PENALTY

Gratian cited St. Isidore (†636) as authority for the statement that a law must be clearly expressed, lest by its obscurity it lead to misunderstanding.[34] Now, in promulgating the fifteenth canon of the II General Council of the Lateran Pope Innocent II was quite clear in the expression he used to indicate those who came within the ambit of the enacted excommunication. He introduced the canon with the words "*Si quis.*" The use of a term which belongs to the category of indefinite pronouns made its extension all-inclusive. Any baptized person, man or woman, layman or clergyman, was made liable for the incurring of the censure.[35] No distinction was made regarding the factor of age. Consequently youths also could fall under the censure, provided, of course, that they had a sufficient use of reason and thus could act responsibly with malicious intent.[36]

In the original canon of the II Lateran Council only the one who physically performed the deed incurred the excommunication. But by the legislation of Alexander III (1159-1181) also the principal authors of the crime *(mandantes)*, the instigators of it *(consulentes)*, and those who gave their consent for it *(consentientes)* were put on a par with the perpetrator of the physi-

delict in question with *iniuria* in Roman Law. The characteristic tendency at the time of the Decretalists to base the concepts of Canon Law upon the authority of the *Corpus Iuris Civilis*, and to explain them with Romanic parallel concepts, led the Decretalists to interpret the phrase "*violentas manus iniicere*" through the Roman concept of *iniuria*. Cf. Kuttner, *Kanonistische Schuldlehre von Gratian bis auf die Dekretalen Gregors IX* (Città del Vaticano: Biblioteca Apostolica Vaticana, 1935), p. 73 (hereafter cited *Schuldlehre)*; Salucci, *Il Diritto Penale* (2 vols., Subiaco: Tipografia dei Monasteri, 1926-1930), II, 170-171; Ayrinhac-Lydon, *Penal Legislation in the New Code of Canon Law* (revised edition, New York: Benziger Brothers, 1936), p. 225; Hollweck, *Die kirchlichen Strafgesetze* (Mainz, 1899), § 148, n. 3.

34 C. 2, D. IV.

35 *Glossa Ordinaria* ad c. 39, C. XVII, q. 4, s. v. "si quis"; c. 6, 7, X, *de sententia excommunicationis*, V, 39.

36 Cf. c. 1, *de sententia excommunicationis*, V, 39.

cal action.[37] The deed, however, had to follow as an actual consequence because of the command, the counsel or the agreement; otherwise no censure was incurred except by the actual perpetrator of the deed.

Pope Innocent III in a letter to the Archbishop of Braga extended the scope of the canon to include a cleric who by intending to offset a previous injury laid violent hands upon some other cleric, even though the latter freely subjected himself to the injury.[38]

Under legislation enacted by Boniface VIII also those who ratified such a crime as well as those who did not impede it became *ipso facto* subject to the excommunication. To ratify the crime meant to approve or to sanction it when committed by another. The duty to impede the crime rested upon everyone who *ex officio* was bound to forestall it. The ones who officially were under obligation to prevent such criminal activity were the kings, the teachers, the pastors, the parents, and the immediate superiors.[39]

Article 8 — The Absolution

The II General Council of the Lateran enacted the first general law in which absolution from a censure was reserved to the Pope.[40] The fifteenth canon of the Council declared that those who were under excommunication for maliciously striking clerics were required to make a journey to Rome to receive the mandate of the Holy See.

By later decretal legislation the law was mitigated to some degree, a distinction being made by Clement III (1187-1191) between a slight or trivial injury and a grave or severe injury. The Pope left it to the discretion of the bishop to decide whether

[37] C. 36, X, *de sententia excommunicationis*, V, 39.

[38] C. 36, X, *de sententia excommunicationis*, V, 39.

[39] C. 23, *de sententia excommunicationis, suspensionis et interdicti*, V, 11, in VI°; c. 1, *de poenis*, V, 8, in Clem.

[40] Moriarity, *The Extraordinary Absolution from Censures*, The Catholic University of America Canon Law Studies, n. 113 (Washington, D. C.:

the injury was grave or slight. If it was slight the bishop himself could absolve. The *Glossa* indicates that it was disputed whether this authorization for the bishop implied a special favor granted by the Pope, or whether it reflected a power bestowed in the common law.[41] Under ordinary circumstances, however, a bishop could not absolve from the excommunication incurred by the one who had inflicted a grave injury. This power was given only in case of necessity or by special concession.[42]

From the express words of the II Lateran Council it was clear that when a repenting delinquent was in danger of death any priest could absolve him from the censure. However, through later legislation by Boniface VIII it became the rule that a person who had been absolved in danger of death by one who under ordinary circumstances could not have absolved him was bound to make the trip to Rome upon his recovery.[43]

From time to time various persons or groups of persons were exempted from making the journey to Rome after they had incurred the censure of the canon. The early commentators formulated the exceptional cases in the following little stanza:

Régula, mórs, sexús, puer, óffíciális,
Déliciósus, inóps, aegérque, senéxque sodális,
Jánitor, ádstrictús, dubiús, causáe, levis fctus,
Débilis ábsolví sine súmma Séde meréntur.[44]

Without adverting to the motives which prompted the exemption of these persons, one may indicate that the following in general were exempt: minors, women, persons who were not

The Catholic University of America, 1938), p. 113; Gross, *Lehrbuch des katholichen Kirchenrechts* (4. ed., Wien, 1903), p. 103.

41 *Glossa Ordinaria,* ad c. 17, X, *de sententia excommunicationis,* V, 39, s. v. "pervenit."

42 Kober, *Der Kirchenbann nach den Grundsätzen des canonischen Rechts* (Tübingen, 1863), p. 490 (hereinafter cited *Kirchenbann).*

43 C. 22, *de sententia excommunicationis, suspensionis et interdicti,* V, 11, in VI°.

44 Panormitanus, *Commentaria in Quinque Libros Decretalium* (5 vols. in 7, Venetiis, 1588), lib. V, tit. xxxix, cap. xxxii, n. 2. Cf. also Barbosa, *Pastoralis Solicitudinis sive de Officio et Potestate Episcopi Descriptio* (3 vols. in 1, Lugduni, 1656), p. 442. Barbosa (1589-1649) attributed these verses to Panormitanus (1386-1453).

sui iuris, the poor, the sick, the crippled and the aged. In addition to these persons there were also those who were impeded from journeying to Rome by reason of their office. Considered to be under a similar disability were the monks and the nuns. Finally, all clerics who lived the community form of life were likewise excused from making the journey to Rome.[45]

Article 9.— Other Penalties Enacted Against Malicious Strikers of Clerics

Thus far consideration has been given solely to the censure of excommunication which was incurred by those who laid violent hands on clerics. But even this penalty, one of the severest within the power of the Church to use against delinquents, did not completely stem the number of crimes committed against the clergy. Boniface VIII, therefore, introduced new measures in an attempt to extirpate these crimes. His Apostolic Constitution was aimed especially at those who molested Cardinals.

The Pope declared that those who imprisoned Cardinals or treated them with violence were guilty of the crime of lèse majesté, and consequently were to be considered perpetually infamous. Furthermore, the guilty one was *ipso facto* deprived of any office as well as of any spiritual or temporal benefice he held in trust from the Church. This privation extended also to descendants in the direct line. The culprit himself and his descendants were under a canonical impediment with respect to the reception of any ecclesiastical orders. To augment the infamy of such a criminal the Pope further directed that he be deprived of the right to partake in legitimate ecclesiastical acts. Pope Boniface expressly indicated that these penalties were to be levied not only on the one who actually perpetrated the violence, but also on his immediate associates. If the death of the Cardinal resulted, then not only the prescriptions of the Constitution were to be observed, but the sanctioned penalties

45 C. 58 and 60; 6 and 13; 26, 58 and 13; 6 and 11, X, *de sententia excommunicationis,* V, 39. This listing of chapters follows the order of the persons listed above.

of the secular powers were to be invoked against the delinquents.[46]

A few years later similar penalties were made applicable to perpetrators of the same delict against bishops. This legislation was made by Pope Clement V (1305-1314) in the General Council which was held at Vienne (1311-1312). The deprivation of benefices, however, extended only to those which the malicious striker held from the bishop whom he struck. Likewise the delinquent's descendants were disqualified for the obtaining of benefices solely in the diocese over which the bishop ruled. Public denunciation of the crime was ordered. If the bishop was imprisoned, his diocese as well as the place in which he was imprisoned was under interdict until he was released.[47]

46 C. 5, *de poenis*, V, 9, in VI°.

47 C. 1, *de poenis*, V, 8, in Clem.

CHAPTER IV

LEGISLATION IN THE PERIOD BETWEEN THE *CORPUS IURIS CANONICI* AND THE COUNCIL OF TRENT

The problem concerning the treatment of those who maliciously assaulted and attacked clergymen caused great concern to the Holy See. The law of the II Lateran Council continued as the prevailing law. Yet from time to time the Popes took occasion to make new regulations in addition to the existing legislation.

Pope Martin V (1417-1431) at the Council of Constance (1414-1418) issued the Constitution *"Ad evitanda"* in which he effected important changes in the penal law. The penal law up to that time indicated that one who was under the ban of excommunication was branded as a *vitandus*.[1] In order to remove the scandals and many dangers which were concomitant with such a policy the Pope changed the law. Thenceforward Catholics were not obliged to avoid contacts and associations with an excommunicate, unless the sentence of excommunication had been rendered, published and denounced by a judge expressly with this effect. But so severe was the penalty for laying violent hands on a cleric that this delict, when notorious, did not share the benefit of the new law. Hence a person who attacked a cleric was likewise to be treated as a *vitandus* if his crime was notorious and could not be concealed by any subterfuge or excused by means of any assistance furnished by the law.[2]

Yet even the severest penalties passed by the Church could not deter some unscrupulous men from violating the personal

1 It may be noted that some exception to the law forbidding communications and associations with excommunicated persons had been made in earlier times. Cf. cc. 102-106, C. XI, q. 3; Rufinus, *Summa Decretorum*, pp. 315-316; Bernardus Papiensis, *Summa Decretalium*, p. 272.

2 Martinus V (in Conc. Constantien.), const. *Ad evitanda*, a. 1418 — *Codicis Iuris Canonici Fontes, cura Emi Petri Card. Gasparri editi* (9 vols., Romae [postea Civitate Vaticana]: Typis Polyglottis Vaticanis, 1923-1939;

rights of clerics. In various countries direct physical attacks were made upon them, or indirect deleterious encroachments upon their health, or upon the enjoyment of the esteem among their flock, which was so essential for the welfare of the Church. Violence of this sort broke out anew in England in the year 1439. It was in that year that Pope Eugene IV (1431-1447) addressed a letter to the Archbishop of Canterbury, in which he indicated that greater and severer penalties should be inflicted in view of the higher dignity which was possessed by prelates in the Church. Those who interfered with the inalienable right of personal security for the Cardinals were guilty of *lèse majesté*. This was not applicable in the case of those who interfered with the sacred rights of patriarchs, archbishops and bishops. Nevertheless, severer punishment was in order in view of their greater dignity over that of priests and lower clerics.[3]

It is unnecessary to dwell on all the minute details of legislation occasioned by the repeated cases which certainly reflected continued abuses. But before the Council of Trent mention should be made of the Constitution *"Supernae dispositionis"* of Leo X (1513-1521) in 1514. In that document the Pope renewed the penalties of his predecessors as enacted against those who violated the persons of Cardinals and Bishops.[4]

Vols. VII-IX, ed. cura et studio Emi Iustiniani Card. Serédi), n. 45. Hereinafter cited *Fontes.*

3 Eugenius IV, ep. *"Non mediocri,"* a. 1439, § 6 — *Fontes,* n. 50.

4 § 40 — *Fontes,* n. 65. Cf. also Leo X (in Conc. Lateranen, V), const. *"Regimini universalis,"* 4 maii 1515, § 11 — *Fontes,* n. 66.

CHAPTER V

FROM THE COUNCIL OF TRENT TO THE PUBLICATION OF THE CODE

ARTICLE 1 — PRELIMINARY NOTATIONS

It may be wondered how the development of this canonical institute through the span of almost four centuries can be disposed of in a single chapter. But there is no incongruity in this, since the legislation enacted prior to the Council of Trent prevailed till the codification of the law in 1917, and at that time was carried over into the Code.[1] Furthermore it is difficult to see how the Church could have made the penalty more severe. She had met the challenge against the personal inviolability of her clergymen by the most severe penalty at her disposal. Even to the present day it has remained as a veritably Draconian law in the penal code.[2]

Although the present chapter takes its starting point from the Council of Trent, no specific details referring to this clerical privilege can be garnered from the Council itself. The Fathers of the Council did not treat *ex professo* of this subject. They did, however, renew and approve the censures that had already emanated from the Apostolic See.[3] By the sixteenth century the malicious assaults on clerics had decreased in number from the

1 Cf. Coronata, *Institutiones Iuris Canonici ad Usum Utriusque Cleri et Scholarum* (5 vols., Vol. IV, Romae: Marietti, 1935), IV, 428. Hereinafter cited *Institutiones.*

2 Lega *(Praelectiones in Textum Iuris Canonici — De Delictis et Poenis* [2. ed., Romae, 1910], p. 218) spoke of excommunication as the penalty "ultra quam Ecclesia non habet amplius quid faciat." He attributed this statement to Pope Celestine III (1191-1198). Celestine wrote: "Sin si depositus incorrigibilis fuerit, excommunicari debet, deinde contumacia crescente anathematis mucrone feriri. Postmodum vero, si in profundum malorum veniens (haec omnia) contempserit, quum Ecclesia non habeat ultra quid faciat, etc." — c. 10, X, *de iudiciis*, II, 1.

3 Conc. Trident., sess. xxv, *de ref.*, c. 12, 20. Cf. Hinschius, *Das Kirchenrecht*, I, 118, n. 3.

peak which they had attained in the preceding centuries. At this period attacks on the Church came in the form of the Protestant "Reformation," and that became the chief concern for legislation from the Holy See.

At most, therefore, only a few conclusions can be drawn from the enactments of the Council on other points. These conclusions were by no means instrumental in effecting radical changes in the discipline hitherto prevailing as regards the privilege of the canon.

Article 2 — Conclusions Drawn from the Council

The privilege of the canon could be considered from a dual aspect, namely, a positive and a negative one. From a positive point of view, the laity were to show to clerics (and this included also all non-clerics who enjoyed the privilege) reverence and obedience in proportion to the dignity and the offices which the clerics held. From a negative point of view, there existed the prohibition against the infliction of bodily harm on clerics. The laws passed by the II Lateran Council under Pope Innocent II, as well as the legislation of the succeeding popes, stressed the negative aspect. This was due in large measure to the contingencies of those times. Rebellious members of the Church did not scruple to vent their wrath on the consecrated members of Christ's Mystical Body, when it suited their imaginary needs to do so.

The Council of Trent, on the other hand, bent as it was on the true reform of both the laity and the clergy, laid emphasis rather on the positive aspect. In the Council the Venerable Fathers issued a special decree on reform which manifested their ardent desire for the restoration of ecclesiastical discipline among the members of the Church, clergy as well as laity.[4] Conscious of the treacheries committed against the clergy in the past, the Council stated that secular princes should be advised of their duty in this regard. Their duty was to permit the rights of the Church to be restored, and to see to it that all their subjects

4 Sess. xxv, *de ref.*, c. 20.

manifested due reverence towards the clergy, especially their parish priests and the higher ecclesiastical superiors. They were not to allow officials or inferior magistrates under their jurisdiction to violate the immunity of the Church and of ecclesiastical persons, which had been established by the authority of God and the ordinances of the sacred canons. For this reason, then, the Council renewed all the established rules of the sacred canons and all the enacted prescriptions of the general councils, as well as all the other Apostolic ordinances which had been published in the interest of ecclesiastical persons.

One cannot but conclude that all the laws already discussed in the preceding chapters of this work had the express approbation of the Council of Trent. That the clergy should reap respect and reverence from the laity was a thing so vital to the preservation of good order in the Church, that the Council put its stamp of approval on all the penal sanctions previously enacted against the violators of the person of clerics. It should be noted that this directive of the Council was primarily aimed at the secular princes. The Council made no specific mention of the faithful in general.

A further observation is in order. The Council spoke of the reverence which was generically due to the clergy *(clerus)*. The term *clerus* is a generic word. Accordingly it included within its ambit all persons within the ecclesiastical hierarchy from the Pope to the one who had received his first tonsure. Over and above this, when reminding bishops of their dignity, the Council commanded that princes as well as others were to pay paternal honor and reverence to bishops in due proportion to their sacred status.[5]

With the sole exception of these passing references to the privilege of the canon, the Council was silent on this point. The Council, however, did single out one occasion on which clerical privileges (among which, of course, was included that of the canon) were forfeited. By the law of the Council the chapter of a Cathedral church was forbidden during the vacancy of a

[5] Sess. xxv, *de ref.*, c. 17.

see to grant permission for ordinations, or to grant dimissorial letters, until the lapse of one year from the vacancy. If in contravention of this decree anyone who was not in straitened circumstances for time with reference to a benefice already granted, or yet to be conferred, nevertheless was advanced to minor orders, he was not to enjoy any clerical privilege.[6] Here, again, the forfeiture of clerical privileges was mentioned simply in a general way, but one can rightfully conclude that with other privileges also the privilege of the canon was rendered forfeit.

Finally, mention should be made of the authority given by the Council of Trent to bishops, whereby they could absolve gratuitously, in the forum of conscience, after the imposition of a salutary penance, either personally or through a vicar especially appointed for this purpose, in all occult cases, even those reserved to the Apostolic See, all delinquents subject to them in their diocese.[7] This faculty was more ample than any similar faculty previously granted in that it included the power to absolve even from those delicts which were reserved to the Holy See for absolution. But this new faculty of the bishops must be carefully analyzed to determine just which cases regarding the excommunication enacted against the *percussores clericorum* could be absolved by the bishop in virtue of this Tridentine faculty.

In the preceding chapter it has been indicated that the only cases reserved for absolution to the pope were those in which there was a *"percussio enormis."* The bishop could absolve in both the internal and the external form from the excommunication entailed through a *"percussio modica et levis."*[8] By virtue of the new Tridentine faculty a bishop could in the forum of conscience absolve his subjects from excommunications incurred through any occult crime.[9] Special emphasis must be put on the fact that the use of the faculty was conditioned on the *occult*

6 Sess. vii, *de ref.*, c. 10.

7 Sess. xxiv, *de ref.*, c. 6.

8 Cf. *supra*, pp. 30-32.

9 Sägmüller, *Lehrbuch des katholischen Kirchenrechts*, Vol. I, Pars III, (Freiburg im Breisgau: Herder Book Co., 1930), p. 337.

nature of the delict. The new grant did not, therefore, include cases wherein the assault was slight, even though public, for the bishop already had the faculty to absolve from the excommunication entailed through such a crime. Nor did it include cases which were only materially, but not also formally, public. Only as long as these latter cases had not found their way before a tribunal, could they be remitted, although perhaps in a strict sense they did not come under occult crimes in the sense of the faculty granted by the Council of Trent.[10] The excommunication incurred through a *"percussio enormis"* could in virtue of the new faculty be absolved if it had remained absolutely occult. Admittedly, as now, so also then, it was difficult to determine in some cases when the assault was grave and when it was only slight. Whenever some doubt was present, then the presumption pointed to a grave assault. St. Alphonsus (1696-1787) taught that the reason for invoking this harsher presumption was to be sought in the Church's concern that no occasion be offered for the perpetration of harm against the ecclesiastical state.[11]

Article 3 — Resolution of Doubts

Although no new legislation was enacted after the Council of Trent relative to the privilege of the canon, it is quite understandable that doubts should arise over such an important question. From time to time questions were proposed to the Sacred Congregation of the Council for solution. But the resolutions of this Congregation did not produce any decisions which were tantamount to effecting a change in the law itself either by extensive or by restrictive interpretation. Indeed, one can easily see that a law to which the sanction of excommunication was attached could give rise to doubts in view of the indicated threefold division of a *"percussio levis, mediocris, et gravis."* It was difficult for anyone to say exactly when a crime of one of these classes was present in contradistinction to that of another class. Yet, this determination was of vast importance since, as has

10 Hollweck, *Die kirchlichen Strafgesetze*, § 148, n. 7.

11 *Theologia Moralis* (cura et studio L. Glaudé, 4 vols., Romae, 1905-1912), lib. VII, n. 280.

already been indicated, the type of crime determined the authority from whom the absolution could be obtained. But even the decisions did not help to establish a universally applicable norm, for very often circumstances were the determining factor in allocating a specific case to a particular class. It will suffice, then, to examine a few of the cases submitted, in order to see whether and within what classification the censure was contracted. But it can be said that the jurisprudence on this point was unaltered by any of the decisions.

1. The Council of Trent had indicated that only those who held an ecclesiastical benefice, or who wore the clerical garb and tonsure, and at the same time served in some church by order of the bishop, or in some school or university on the way, as it were, to the reception of major Orders, enjoyed the privilege of the forum.[12] This gave rise to the question whether an unmarried cleric who did not possess a benefice and who refused to wear the ecclesiastical garb thereby forfeited the privilege of the canon. But in February, 1589, the Sacred Congregation of the Council replied that such a delinquent was not *eo ipso* deprived of the protection granted by the privilege of the canon.[13]

But even after this many still taught that all clerical privileges were lost. Finally a case was brought by certain clerics of the Archdiocese of Chieti to the Sacred Congregation of the Council. The Archbishop, basing his decisions on a diocesan statute passed by his predecessor, had declared these clerics deprived of all clerical privileges for their refusal to wear the tonsure and the clerical garb. On June 10, 1684, the Sacred Congregation, in answering the recourse, merely declared that they had lost only the privilege of the forum. It made no mention of the validity or invalidity of the statute. The specific decision as made in this response could hardly have been unexpected, for the matter was one which related to penal law, and hence a strict interpretation of the words of the Council of Trent was to be expected.[14]

12 Sess. xxiii, *de ref.*, c. 6.

13 Benedictus XIV, *De Synodo Dioecesana,* lib. XII, c. 2, n. I.

14 Benedictus XIV, *ibidem,* n. II.

The question was solved. Those who did not wear the tonsure or the clerical habit did not lose the privilege of the canon. This discipline prevailed until the year 1860. At that time the Sacred Congregation of Ecclesiastical Immunity decreed that all those clerics, not in sacred Orders, who lost the privilege of the forum for their refusal to obey the prescription of the Council of Trent in this matter lost also the privilege of the canon.[15] From then on all such clerics *ipso iure et facto* lost the protection of this privilege, and also the privileges concomitant with the order they had received. No admonition or declaration of the judge was necessary.[16]

2. In the year 1639 the Holy Office indicated that the clerical privileges, especially that of the canon, extended to the Greek priests.[17] On the same occasion the Holy Office indicated that Latins who laid violent hands on a Greek priest fell under the censure of excommunication.

3. A certain bishop had a doubt whether he could absolve from the excommunication incurred through a *"percussio mediocris"* if the case had been brought to the contentious forum. In replying to the bishop, the Sacred Congregation of the Council indicated that the faculty given to bishops by the Council of Trent had in no way modified the faculties granted to bishops by the Decretal law. By the law of the Decretals a bishop could absolve his subject from the excommunication when it was incurred through an assault of an intermediate nature.[18] By this decision, however, it became patent that bishops enjoyed the

15 Die 20 Septembris 1860 — *Acta Sanctae Sedis* (41 vols., Romae, 1865-1908), III (1867), 433.

16 Cf. Aichner, *Compendium Juris Ecclesiastici* (6. ed., Brixinae, 1887), p. 232.

17 The term "Greek priests" was used in the following question submitted to the Holy Office: "Se i sacerdoti greci, massime cattolici, godano i privilegi che si godano dai latini, e particularmente de canone *Si quis suadente etc.*" R. "Quoad privilegium Canonis, affirmative." — *Fontes*, n. 726.

18 C. 17, X, *de sententia excommunicationis*, V, 39.

power of absolving according to Decretal law, even when the case was brought to court.[19]

4. At times it was found necessary to declare the sentence of excommunication on delinquents. This, of course, involved the question of jurisdiction. In the year 1719 the Archbishop of Milan was enmeshed in a difficulty of this kind. In his Archdiocese the Monks of Mt. Olivet had the vested care of a parish church. There was, however, great contention, jealousy and argumentation between the perpetual vicar, who had the actual care of the parish, and the monks at the monastery. Finally two monks maliciously assaulted the vicar, as a result of which judicial proceedings were held in the court of the Archbishop. These proceedings were called into question because it was doubtful that the Archbishop had jurisdiction in the case. An appeal was made to the Sacred Congregation of the Council, which held that the Curia of the Archbishop could declare the excommunication or at least denounce the excommunicated monks.[20]

Article 4 — The Constitution *Apostolicae Sedis*

Due to the great number of *latae sententiae* penalties, to the doubts and anxieties arising therefrom, and to the fact that many of these had lost their meaning, Pius IX (1846-1878) introduced a change in the penal discipline previously prevailing. Upon the enactment of the Constitution *Apostolicae Sedis* of 1869 only those censures retained their force which were expressly mentioned therein. This Constitution had the character of a universal Church law, and had as its goal the reformation of previously existing penal law. The new law was concerned only with *latae sententiae* censures, and therefore all vindicative penalties retained their force.[21]

After indicating the *raison d'être* for the new law, the Pope

19 ——————, "Privilège du Clergé," — *Analecta Juris Pontificii* (Romae, 1855-1869; Parisiis, 1872-1891), Vol. IV, Pars 2 (1866), 1827.

20 *Fontes,* n. 3194.

21 *Fontes,* n. 552.

enumerated the *latae sententiae* censures which thereafter were to prevail. According to the customary method a division was made among the censures as being reserved to the Pope, as being reserved to the bishop, and as not being reserved to anyone. Then a new division was introduced, namely, one that distinguished between censures reserved *speciali modo* and censures reserved *simplici modo* to the Roman Pontiff. This latter distinction adverted to the case in which there existed the power to absolve on the part of the one who enjoyed general faculties. The one who was given a general concession of absolving from cases and censures reserved to the Pope could not in virtue simply of this concession absolve from cases and censures which were *speciali modo* reserved to the Roman Pontiff. Such a general concession, however, sufficed for absolving from cases and censures which were *simplici modo* reserved to the Roman Pontiff.[22]

Over and above the list of censures drawn up in the Constitution, all those censures retained their force which were passed by the Council of Trent.[23] But the Pope did not wish to reaffirm those censures which the Council of Trent had approved and renewed from the *Jus Novum*.[24] Also remaining in force were censures relating to the criminal acts perpetrated in connection with the election of the pope, and with reference to the internal rule of religious orders, institutes, certain colleges, etc.[25]

Finally, the Pope reaffirmed the faculty granted by the Council of Trent whereby bishops could absolve in the forum of conscience from penalties incurred through occult crimes. His express mention of this faculty may be due to the fact that he wished to exclude from that faculty the power to absolve censures reserved in a special manner to the Roman Pontiff.

In the list of censures there are contained two which concern

22 Const. *Apostolicae Sedis*, § I, in fine — *Fontes*, n. 552. Cf. Santi-Leitner, *Praelectiones Juris Canonici* (4. ed., 5 vols. in 3, Ratisbonae-Romae, 1903-1905), lib. V, tit. 39, n. 23.

23 Const. *Apostolicae Sedis*, §§ IV; VI, n. 2.

24 This phrase is here used in the sense adopted by the *"Praefatio"* to the new Code. It includes, therefore, all the laws from the time of Gratian to the time of the Council of Trent.

25 Const. *Apostolicae Sedis*, § VI. Cf. Aichner, *op. cit.*, p. 730.

the violation of the privilege of the canon. The first case is reserved to the Pope in a special manner, the second in a simple manner. The two paragraphs read as follows:

1. "Omnes interficientes, mutilantes, percutientes, capientes, carcerantes, detinentes, vel hostiliter insequentes S. R. E. Cardinales, Patriarchos, Archiepiscopos, Episcopos, Sedisque Apostolicae Legatos, vel Nuncios, aut eos a suis Dioecesibus, Territoriis, Terris seu Dominiis eiicientes, nec non ea mandantes, vel rata habentes, seu praestantes in eis auxilium, consilium vel favorem."[26]
2. "Violentas manus, suadente diabolo, iniicientes in Clericos, vel utriusque sexus Monachos, exceptis quoad reservationem casibus et personis, de quibus iure vel privilegio permittitur, ut Episcopus aut alius absolvat."[27]

A comparative study of these two sections indicates that they retained the discipline that was in force up to that time. The law which is stated in the first paragraph is similar to the penalty levied by the II General Council of the Lateran (1139), and has a wording similar to that used by Clement V (1305-1314) in the General Council of Vienne (1311-1312) in the enactments which were aimed at those who molested archbishops and bishops.[28]

The second paragraph practically restates the law as it was first published by Innocent II (1130-1143). The conclusion, therefore, is that the penalty incurred through malicious assaults on clerics was left intact by this new Constitution. Consequently all the details discussed in the preceding chapters relating to the privilege of the canon still remained in effect after the appearance of the Constitution *Apostolicae Sedis.* The regal dignity of the cleric, which receives its crown in the priesthood, continued to be treasured and protected by the Church with all the means at her disposal.

26 Const. *Apostolicae Sedis,* § I, n. 5 — *Fontes,* n. 552.

27 *Ibidem,* § II, n. 2 — *Fontes,* n. 552.

28 C. 1, *de poenis,* V, 8, in Clem. Cf. *supra,* p. 33.

CANONICAL COMMENTARY

CHAPTER VI

CLERICAL PRIVILEGES

Article 1 — Respect for the Clergy

A. Distinction between Clergy and Laity

In founding His Church, Christ did not communicate the power which He had received from His Father to all the faithful, but rather to a certain group, His Apostles and their successors. Thus, juridically, the Church has by divine command been organized as an unequal society.[1] Authority, indeed, is necessary for juridical societies. Dependent upon whether the authority is vested in all the members or only in one or several, societies are divided into equal and unequal societies. In an equal society the exercise of any authority demands the consent of all, whereas in an unequal society the head of the society can wield his authority independently of his subjects.[2] Because of its hierarchic[3] constitution, one essential feature found in the Church is the distinction between the clergy and the laity. The Code in canon 107 restates this principle of divine law.[4] Those entering the Church are bound to obey ecclesiastical superiors, and the recalcitrant can be properly punished.

1 Chelodi, *Ius de Personis iuxta Codicem Iuris Canonici* (ed. altera a Sac. Ernesto Bertagnolli recognita et aucta, Tridenti: Libr. Edit. Tridentum, 1927), p. 10.

2 Coronata, *Ius Publicum Ecclesiasticum* (2. ed., Taurini: Marietti, 1934), n. 17.

3 The term "hierarchic" is used in a broad sense to indicate the power which Christ left to His Apostles and their successors to rule and sanctify the faithful. Cf. Chelodi, *op. cit.*, p. 11; Coronata, *op. cit.*, n. 40, 2°.

4 "Ex divina institutione sunt in Ecclesia *clerici a laicis* distincti, licet non omnes clerici sint divinae institutionis; utrique autem possunt esse *religiosi.*"

B. *Respect for the Clergy*

The clergy by divine ordinance have in the Church a position of preeminence, for to that body has been given the charge of ruling and sanctifying the faithful. Since clergymen are by reason of their position to wield in the Church the authority entrusted to them by Christ, respect and reverence for their office is mandatory from the faithful. In a well-ordered society the relationship between superiors and inferiors enjoins respect for authority. But the faithful owe reverence and respect to a cleric, not only because of the office which he holds, but also because of the sacred nature of the clerical state itself.[5]

This special prerogative whereby clerics are entitled to special reverence and respect from the faithful at large is known as the privilege of the canon. This terminology is not employed by the legislator in the Code of Canon Law, but the principles of this privilege are enunciated in canons 119 and 2343. That this privilege can be considered from a dual aspect, i. e., from a positive as well as a negative aspect, has already been considered in the historical synopsis.[6]

It can be noted here that the positive obligation of reverence, varying in accordance with the rank of the cleric in the hierarchy of orders or of jurisdiction, is found expressed in the words of canon 119: "*Omnes fideles debent clericis, pro diversis eorum gradibus et muneribus, reverentiam* . . ." After analyzing the history of this privilege one may rightly conclude that it will be only rarely that a grave fault will be committed through the neglect to manifest special signs of reverence to the clergy. Therefore, the practical importance of the privilege is mainly concerned with the negative aspect, whereby actions derogatory to the honor due to the clerical state are prohibited. Such an action assumes the malice of sacrilege, as is clear from canon 119: ". . . *seque sacrilegii delicto commaculant, si quando clericis realem iniuriam intulerint.*" Although verbal injury to

5 Ferreres, *Institutiones Canonicae* (2. ed., 2 vols., Barcinone: Subirana, 1920), I, 100.

6 *Supra*, p. 37.

clerics constitutes a crime punishable by the law,[7] only real (physical) injury is meant when the privilege of the canon is mentioned, as is patent from the legislation of the canon to which reference has just been made.

There is no obligation on the part of the laity to extend equal reverence to all clerics. The reverence and respect owed admits of gradation in proportion to the cleric's position in the hierarchy of orders or of jurisdiction.[8]

It is commonly taught by authors that the word *gradus* of canon 119 has reference to the rank in the hierarchy of orders, and the word *munus* refers to rank in the hierarchy of jurisdiction.[9] However, the use of these same words is not so restricted in other sections of the Code. In canon 106, 3°, for example, *gradus* clearly refers to rank in the hierarchy of jurisdiction in the clause: *"inter eiusdem gradus personas sed non eiusdem ordinis."* In a similar manner, the term *munus* does not always indicate an office to which is annexed jurisdiction. A notary, for example, does not necessarily have jurisdiction, yet canon 2037, § 1, speaks of his office as a *munus.* But since this distinction of the authors presents no legal difficulties it may well be adopted.

C. *Clerical Prerogatives Arising from the Privilege of the Canon*

The clerical state and the reception of orders gives to clerics a certain dignity and excellence which of necessity must be

7 Canons 2344; 2355.

8 It would not be apropos of this dissertation to enter into a discussion concerning the nature and divisions of the hierarchy. It is sufficient to note that the hierarchy (understood subjectively) consists of the group of clerics to whom some ecclesiastical power has been given in distinct and subordinate degrees. The hierarchy of orders consists of bishops, priests, and ministers; the hierarchy of jurisdiction of the supreme pontificate and of the episcopate. Cf. canon 108, § 2. For a more detailed study regarding the hierarchy and its various aspects the reader is referred to Wernz-Vidal, *Ius de Personis*, nn. 47-55.

9 Ojetti, *Commentarium in Codicem Iuris Canonici* (4 vols., Romae: apud Aedes Universitatis Gregorianae, 1927-1931), lib. II, ad can. 119, n. 2 (hereafter this work will be cited as *Commentarium); ;* Beste, *Introductio in Codicem* (ed. altera, Collegeville, Minn.: St. John's Abbey Press, 1944), p. 176.

acknowledged in some external manner. This will, of course, vary with local conditions and customs, but an indication can be given of some of the ways in which this respect can, and in some cases must, be shown. First, a cleric has the right to be held in esteem by the laity. Tipping the hat and rising in the presence of a priest are signs of respect. Furthermore, clergymen of higher rank are entitled to respect from the lesser clerics. Thus, the obeisance of a priest to his bishop is a sign of regard for his higher position. Secondly, clerics because of their privilege may receive certain honorary titles such as: Your Holiness, Your Eminence, Your Excellency, Your Reverence, etc. Thirdly, the clergy have a right to a nobler place in the Church. Thus there has arisen the custom of erecting a choir for the use of the clergy. Likewise in ecclesiastical processions and meetings the clergy takes precedence over the laity.

Fourthly, the clergy has a right to canonical obedience from the laity. This is especially so in the case of clerics who are exercising the authority of jurisdiction vested in them. In the juridical order the Roman Pontiff is the head and ordinary pastor of all the faithful, clergy and laity alike; the local ordinary is the ecclesiastical ruler of his territory and of those subject to him. Persistent disobedience to them is subversive of the hierarchic order and constitutes in the present law a special delict.[10] Good order in society demands that inferiors obey their lawful superiors. Hence the clergy have a right to the obedience of the laity when they give a legitimate command.[11]

Article 2 — General Notions Concerning Privileges

A. *Preliminary Notions*

The superiority of the clerical state over the lay state is manifested by certain external signs which constitute the rights and privileges of clerics. The privilege of the canon, the canonical institute whose origin and development is under discussion

10 Canon 2331.

11 Cocchi, *Commentarium in Codicem Iuris Canonici* (8 vols. in 5, Taurinorum Augustae: Marietti, 1930-1940), lib. II, pars I, sec. 1, n. 31 (hereafter cited as *Commentarium*).

in this dissertation, is one of the clerical privileges. Canon 119 which enunciates this privilege comes under the title whose caption reads: *"De iuribus et privilegiis clericorum."*[12] Some authors[13] in commenting on this title aver that rights are reducible to privileges insofar as they grant favors. Hence they conclude that rights and privileges have a synonymous signification.

This indiscriminate identification of terms, however, does not seem to be warranted, for the rubrics of the title clearly imply a distinction between the two.[14] While it is true that privileges confer a right, it cannot be held that a clerical right constitutes a privilege, for clerics have a right, not a privilege, to obtain ecclesiastical benefices and pensions.[15] Coronata, drawing a line of demarcation between the two, considers clerical rights as so intimately connected with the clerical state that it is impossible to conceive the state without them. The clerical state without privileges, however, is easily conceivable. Furthermore the rights of clerics cannot be lost, for they depend on the indelible character imprinted by ordination.[16] The clerical privileges can be lost in the various ways delineated in the law.[17] As a final argument, it may be noted that the Code refers to the clerical privileges contained in canons 119 to 123,[18] excluding thereby any

12 Canons 119 to 123 are under this title.

13 Wernz-Vidal, *Ius de Personis*, n. 69; Augustine, *A Commentary on the New Code of Canon Law* (8 vols., St. Louis: Herder Book Co., 1925-1938; Vol. II, 6. ed., 1936), II, 56 (hereafter cited *A Commentary on Canon Law)*.

14 The principle, *"A rubro ad nigrum valet argumentum,"* can still be used to some advantage in the present law. This adage indicates that an argument from the rubrics or title of a statute, which was anciently written in red letters, to the law itself is valid, provided that the red does not contradict the black, i.e., the law. Cf. Lijdsman, *Introductio in Jus Canonicum* (2 vols., Hilversum in Hollandia: Sumptibus Societatis Editricis Pontificiae Anonymae, 1924-1929), I, 266; Cicognani, *Canon Law*, p. 610.

15 Canon 118.

16 Coronata, *Institutiones*, I, 210; 215.

17 Examples of this may be found in canons 123; 132, § 2; 141; 136, § 3; 669, § 2; 2304, § 2; 2305, § 1.

18 Cf. canons 614 and 680.

reference to canon 118. If the terms "rights" and "privileges" were used interchangeably, there would have been no reason for excluding canon 118. It should not, therefore, be presumed that the word *et* in this title is to be understood as a copulative for joining synonymous words.

To clarify the distinction between the two concepts, a definition of both is in order. Clerical rights are special subjective faculties possessed by clerics whereby they are enabled to perform some positive action, or to demand something which does not rest within any rightful claim on the side of the laity.[19] These rights are usually referred to as prerogatives. Clerical privileges, on the other hand, are favors. It may be said that they constitute the title by reason of which clerics are exempt from the common obligations and offices of lay persons. These are commonly referred to as clerical exemptions or immunities. As has been noted in the historical synopsis, the privilege of the canon is one of the personal immunities of clerics.[20]

B. *Definition and Divisions of Privileges*

1. Definition:

Thus far frequent mention has been made of the clerical privileges, and specifically of the privilege of the canon. To what extent the principles of privilege according to the Code of Canon Law apply to the clerical privileges must now be determined.[21]

The English word "privilege" has been taken over from the Latin word *privilegium,* which etymologically is compounded from the Latin adjective *privus* and the noun *lex. Lex,* of course, signifies "law," and *privus* indicates something "singular or individual." [22] The resultant in English would be "a law for individual persons or groups."

19 Beste, *Introductio in Codicem,* p. 175.

20 *Supra,* p. 2; cf. also Coronata, *Ius Publicum Ecclesiasticum,* n. 147.

21 In the treatment of this point reference will frequently be made to the privileges contained in the Code of Canon Law, or to the clerical privileges in general. Since the privilege of the canon falls into both of these categories it must always be understood to be included.

22 Ernout-Meillet, *Dictionnaire Étymologique de la Langue Latine* (Paris: Librairie C. Klinchsieck, 1932), s. v. "privus."

Before giving a formal definition of privilege, one must note that the Code employs the term in a dual sense. The basis for this twofold usage is to be found in the source of privileges. All privileges owe their origin either to a legal concession according to the norms of canon 63, § 1,[23] or to the enactments of the law itself. The former are privileges in the strict sense of the term; the latter can be called privileges only in a broad sense, and are referred to in the Code as *privilegia in Codice contenta.*[24] These two types of privileges have this in common, that both contain favors either against or beyond the law and both are presumed to be perpetual.[25]

Many and varied definitions of privilege have been given during the long history of Canon Law. Yet no authentic definition has been embodied in the law itself. In one of his Decretals Pope Innocent III (1198-1216) had described a privilege as a private law.[26] An examination of this Decretal indicates that the Pope did not intend to give a definition of privilege. His statement might rather be classed as an *obiter dictum* in the solution which he gave to a case regarding the contentions of two abbeys relative to the appointment of an Abbot.

The formulation of a definition has been left to the commentators on Canon Law. Because of the complexities involved in putting all the elements into a simple definition, authors have not been in absolute agreement on a definition. A definition which seems to include most of the constitutive elements of a

23 Canon 63, § 1: "Privilegia acquiri possunt non solum per directam concessionem competentis auctoritatis et per communicationem, sed etiam per legitimam consuetudinem aut praescriptionem."

24 Canon 71. Examples of these privileges are the privileges of clerics (canons 119-123), the privileges of Cardinals (canon 239), of bishops (canon 349), etc. The use of the phrase "*privilegia in Codice contenta*" does not preclude the possibility of other privileges in a wide sense being granted by law though not contained in the Code. — Regatillo, *Institutiones Iuris Canonici* (2 vols., Santander: Sal Terrae, 1941-1942), I, 92. Cf. Beste, *Introductio in Codicem*, p. 485.

25 Cf. canon 70.

26 C. 25, X, *de verborum significatione*, V, 40.

privilege has been given by Roelker.[27] Accepting most of the elements of Sanguinetti's (1829-1893)[28] definition, he defines a privilege as a concession of some special right made by a competent superior. He prefers this definition insofar as the nature of a privilege is correctly described as a concession. Of its very nature a privilege implies that the beneficiary has the option of accepting or rejecting the provision. This notion is emphasized in the definition. This definition is also recommended because it indicates that a privilege grants a right which is otherwise unattainable, either in itself or in its permanence. It likewise lays stress on the note of specialty and the competence of the superior granting the privilege.

This definition of privilege, however, cannot easily be made applicable to privileges in a wide sense, since the liberty to accept or reject them is not given to those who enjoy them. If in the definition the concession is understood to be a grant which prescinds from the liberty of the grantee to accept or to reject the privilege, then the definition may also be used with reference to privileges in the broad sense. Also, it may well be argued that a person freely embraces the state or office to which these privileges attach, and consequently also voluntarily accepts the privileges annexed thereto. However, to preclude any difficulty it is better to seek a special definition of this group of privileges.

Coronata gives a definition of a privilege as understood in a broad sense which may well be adopted. He defines a privilege as a "ius singulare favorabile contra vel praeter ius, determinato personarum ordini vel coetui aut etiam locis et rebus ad modum legis legitime constitutum et promulgatum."[29] This definition seems to embody all the elements whereby a privilege in a wide sense is distinguished from a strict privilege. In this definition Coronata classifies such a privilege as a *ius singulare*. The *ius singulare* is an institution taken over from the Roman Law of

27 *Principles of Privilege according to the Code of Canon Law*, The Catholic University of America Canon Law Studies, n. 35 (Washington, D. C.: The Catholic University of America, 1926), p. 16. In this work an analysis of the traditional definitions of privilege is given.

28 *Institutiones Iuris Ecclesiastici Privati* (Romae, 1884), p. 71.

29 *Institutiones*, I, 95.

the Classic Age.[30] It was in Roman Law a common privilege constituted by a true law for special classes of persons for some special advantage. The *ius singulare* later became incorporated in succeeding codifications of law. This institute of the Roman jurists corresponds to the institution of privileges in a broad sense as known in Canon Law.

That a privilege is something exceptional and favorable is also indicated in the definition given by Coronata. Privileges in a broad sense, besides being privileges, are also, as the definition indicates, true laws. Consequently, all the prescripts of the Code regarding laws must be applied to these privileges. The proper subject of a group privilege is a class of persons who are proper subjects of law. These privileges, being real laws, follow the necessity of law and hence must be promulgated. The rule regarding the period of abeyance before a law operates with binding effect, as determined in canon 9, is also applicable to them. Furthermore, knowledge of such privileges is always presumed, and there is no need to prove their existence in court.[31]

Since privileges in a wide sense are both laws and privileges, they must be interpreted in the light of the principles governing both of these institutes, provided there is no conflict of principles. If, however, the privileges of these two institutes in their application to privileges of this type cannot be reconciled, then the norm for the interpretation of law must prevail. So, v. g., canon 50, which establishes a norm for the settlement of doubts about rescripts (also to be applied to privileges according to canon 68), cannot be used to resolve doubts about privileges in a wide sense.[32]

30 Leonhard, *Institutionen des römischen Rechts* (Leipzig, 1894), p. 24. Cf. Michiels, *Normae Generales Iuris Canonici* (2 vols., Lublin: Universitas Catholica, 1929), II, 308 (hereafter cited as *Normae Generales).*

31 Coronata, *Institutiones*, I, 95.

32 Vermeersch-Creusen, *Epitome Iuris Canonici* (3 vols., Mechliniae-Romae: H. Dessain, 1934-1937; Vol. I, 6. ed., 1937), I, 155 (hereafter cited *Epitome);* Michiels, *Normae Generales*, II, 356-357.

2. Divisions of Privileges:

For the purpose of clarity it seems warranted here to list the divisions of privileges which are particularly referable to privileges in a broad sense. A division based on a consideraton of the passive subject of privileges distinguishes them into personal and real privileges. A personal privilege is one which is granted to some physical or moral person. If the privilege is granted directly in favor of a person because of his own merit it is *individually* personal. But if it is granted to some class of persons the members of which enjoy the privilege only because they belong to the class, it is *jointly* personal. The clerical privileges are of this latter type. Real privileges attach to some object, place or office. Indirectly these privileges are personal insofar as the person to whom the object, place or office belongs exercises the right to the use of the privilege.[33]

If the source of privileges is considered, privileges may be viewed in an efficient sense and in a subjective sense. Strict privileges are a concession embodying a favor. In an efficient sense it is the provision itself which is called a privilege. In a subjective sense the privilege is the favor contained in the grant. This division can also be applied to privileges in a broad sense. In an efficient sense the privilege is the law by which the favor is granted. In a subjective sense it is the favor itself which is the privilege.[34]

Finally, a division may be made as deriving from the purpose served by the privileges. In this light privileges may be either private or common. A private privilege primarily and inherently considers the good of particular persons, and only indirectly looks to the good of the community. Thus, the *restitutio in integrum*[35] as permitted to minors directly affects the good of minors, but ultimately works to the good of the community. A common privilege is one which primarily and inherently aims at the common good of the community at large, although it ultimately

33 Regatillo, *Institutiones Iuris Canonici,* I, 92.

34 Roelker, *Principles of Privilege according to the Code of Canon Law,* p. 30.

35 Canon 1687.

also redounds to the advantage of the members of the society. Thus the privilege of the canon is the legal protection afforded clerics as a class or group against real (physical) injury. Ultimately this works to the weal of the individual clerics, since it engenders reverence for the clergy and respect for authority.[36]

C. Application of the Foregoing Principles to the Privilege of the Canon

It has been shown in the historical synopsis that the designation "privilege of the canon" owes its origin to the famous fifteenth canon of the II General Council of the Lateran (1139). The primary purpose of this canon was to enact a penalty against those who inflicted malicious real (physical) injury on clerics and monks. Consequently, reference to this canon as a clerical privilege seems to be an anomaly. The canon of the II General Council of the Lateran does not make any positive grant to clerics. The fact that those who lay violent hands on clerics incur an excommunication can scarcely be called a clerical privilege. The terminology, however, has survived the test of time, and should be preserved. But a title such as "excommunication of the canon" or "penalty of the canon"—titles employed in the Decretal Law—much more aptly describes this legislation. With regard to this enactment one must bear in mind that the Church was giving official recognition to the sacredness of the clerical state. Owing to the exigencies of those times, however, it was necessary for the Church to lay emphasis on the negative aspect of the privilege. So true is this that even to the present day when reference is made to the privilege, one thinks of it as the juridic institute which forbids the perpetration of malicious injury to clerics, and abstracts from the positive obligation of manifesting reverence towards the clergy. It is really the posi-

36 Wernz-Vidal, *Ius Canonicum,* I, n. 290, *in fine.* Other divisions of privileges have been omitted, since they do not directly pertain to the topic under discussion. For further divisions of privileges the reader is referred to the works already cited and to other canonical works containing a treatise on privileges.

tive aspect behind the legislation which constitutes the privilege. The excommunication is not the privilege itself, but is rather the protection which serves to secure for clerics the enjoyment of their privilege.

It cannot be gainsaid that the privilege of the canon is a real privilege, for all the essential elements of a privilege can be found therein. In any privilege there must first of all be contained some favor. Privileges, it is true, may be burdensome to others[37] and there may even be some obligation incumbent on the beneficiary of the privilege,[38] but the privilege itself must always confer some benefit. Thus by the privilege of the canon clerics are given the favor of personal inviolability. In order to have a privilege the favor must be something special and exceptional. Roelker says that this specialty is so necessary for privileges that without it they would be unintelligible.[39] In a subjective sense, indeed, the privilege of the canon cannot be considered as being special, for under this aspect it must be considered as a true law, not as a strict privilege. In an efficient sense, however, the favor granted by the privilege of the canon can be considered as having the note of specialty inasmuch as for its very existence a special concession of the legislator was required.[40]

Another element can also be noted. The privilege of the canon, like other privileges contained in the law, is a private law, i. e., a law for a particular class of persons, and as such constitutes a new norm of objective law. For those persons who enjoy its benefits, the privilege itself takes the place of the law. Hence a cleric is bound to demand the respect owed to him, and he is never permitted to renounce the privilege.[41] The question of the renunciation of the privilege of the canon will be treated more fully in the following article.

37 Canon 76.

38 Canon 1448.

39 *Principles of Privilege according to the Code of Canon Law,* p. 16.

40 Cf. Michiels, *Normae Generales,* II, 320; 323. In the historical synopsis it was shown that the privilege of the canon is of ecclesiastical origin, although it has its basis in the divine law. — *Supra,* pp. 1-3.

41 Cf. Michiels, *op. cit.,* II, 32.

Article 3 — Renunciation of the Privilege of the Canon Forbidden

Persons enjoying the privilege of the canon are never free to renounce it.[42] To renounce the privilege would be tantamount to a refusal on one's own authority to accept a legal obligation which has been imposed by competent authority for the common good. As has already been indicated, the privilege is a real law and as such can cease to bind only by the will of the legislator. The privilege of the canon, since it is one of the *jointly* personal privileges, cleaves to the individual cleric but belongs to the clergy as a class. It cannot be waived by any private agreement. Through a malicious, physical injury committed against a cleric it is the Church that is harmed more than the individual cleric.[43]

In one of the Decretals of Pope Innocent III (1198-1216) there was express legislation to forbid the renunciation of the privilege of the canon.[44] The Archbishop of Braga had written to the Pope to ask about the juridical import of a custom in his archdiocese whereby clerics, when they had been guilty of injuring another person, voluntarily submitted to a beating as satisfaction. Frequently this beating was administered by laymen. The Archbishop sought to know whether the one administering the punishment fell under the excommunication enacted by the II General Council of the Lateran against those who maliciously strike clerics. The Pope replied that the flogging did not constitute a violent assault, but was injurious to the clerical state, since the canon was enacted not so much in favor of the individual cleric as in favor of the clerical state. Hence it was forbidden, and future violations after episcopal prohibition were to be punished with excommunication.

From this reply the principle can be formulated that a voluntary submission to injurious humiliating assault is forbidden for the reason that the sustaining of such treatment is indecorous to the clerical state. According to the teaching of the *Glossa,* when

42 Canons 72, § 4; 123.

43 C. 15, X, *de sententia excommunicationis,* V, 39.

44 C. 36, X, *de sententia excommunicationis,* V, 39.

there was question of the laying of violent hands on clerics, not only the factor of violence, but also the factors of foolhardiness and injury claimed consideration.[45] This Decretal has been treated here in the canonical commentary, since it so clearly delineates the fact that not only the action which draws excommunication upon its perpetrator, but also any injurious action which reflects unfavorably on the clerical state is forbidden.

With regard to the question of renunciation several practical problems may now be treated. The first concerns clerics who volunteer to submit to a hazing which constitutes part of an initiation ceremonial. Such an initiation is often required for admission into fraternities, lodges, etc. The question can become a very practical one in the case of chaplains in the armed forces who cross the equator for the first time. According to a custom existing among those in the service, those who cross the equatorial line for the first time are submitted to a type of hazing. These ceremonies frequently call for some kind of penalties, such as paddling, immersion in a tub of water, etc. It cannot, however, be said that a cleric is relinquishing the privilege of the canon by submitting to such an initiation. It is true that the blows received in this initiation may be more severe than those received from one striking the cleric maliciously. However, the initiation is all done in a spirit of fun and without any degradation of the clerical state. For this reason, then, a violation of the privilege of the canon is precluded. There may, of course, be circumstances and times when such an action on the part of a cleric would be inadvisable, but still the act would not constitute a violation of the privilege of the canon.

A second and perhaps more complex problem is that of boxing. If clerics engage in boxing merely for the sake of the sport and skill involved, there is no violation of the privilege of the canon. The match can be engaged in as a form of sports, not as a means of settling some grudge, for certainly the principle that

45 "Nota quod in iniectione manuum non solum violentia attenditur, sed etiam temeritas et iniuria" — *Glossa Ordinaria* ad c. 36, X, *de sententia excommunicationis*, V, 39, s. v. "contingit."

mutual injury is admitted as compensation[46] has no application when the privilege of the canon is in question. From the question of boxing one is led to the question of prize-fighting. Prize-fighting is boxing on a more elaborate scale. Hence as far as the principles regulating the privilege of the canon are concerned the same holds true for prize-fighting as for boxing.[47] However, to the present writer it seems incontrovertible that this is an occupation which is unbecoming the clerical state and thus is forbidden to clerics by the law of canon 138.

Finally, a few remarks are in order about field games engaged in by clerics. Frequently these games are keenly contested. There is connected with most games of sport a certain amount of roughness and personal contact with other players. It is not unusual for players to be injured or rendered unconscious as a result of the play. When a cleric engages in and enjoys these games, it cannot be said that he forfeits his privilege of personal inviolability during the game. These field games are always played for the sport involved. It would be wrong to conclude that an injury suffered by a cleric in this form of recreation was the result of a malicious onslaught and inflicted with a view to the degradation of the clerical state. The overall purpose of the privilege of the canon is more to protect and foster respect for the clerical state than to protect the cleric himself from injury. It was never intended that clerics should be obliged to abstain from this legitimate means of recreation even though the blows be more severe than when they are maliciously struck.

An analogous case was recently solved by a writer in a current periodical.[48] A perplexed novice master had doubts about the lawfulness of heated matches between novices and postulants. In the course of the game some of the novices were excluded

46 Canon 2218, § 3.

47 For the Moral Theology on this point cf., v. g., Aertyns-Damen, *Theologia Moralis* (13. ed. [5. ed. post Codicem], 2 vols., Taurini-Romae: Marietti, 1939), I, n. 586, 5°.

48 Fallon, "The Privilege of the Canon"—*Irish Ecclesiastical Record* (Dublin, 1864—), 5. series, LI (1938), 76.

from the game because there was an infraction of the rules of the game which constituted what is nowadays referred to as a "foul." The referee in the game was obliged to invoke the penalty, which was disqualification of the player. The novice master argued that, although the blow was dealt under the influence of sudden impulse or anger, there was no mitigation of the penalty demanded by the rules of the game, i. e., the disqualification of the player. He felt, therefore, that the same held true for the penalty of excommunication to be incurred *ipso facto* for the striking of clerics, at least to the extent that the penalty was enforceable in the external forum.

In solving the case the writer indicated that robust play is inevitable in games played by mortals. If an occasional blow is struck in the heat of the conflict it cannot be presumed that the elements requisite for constituting a delict punishable by the Code are present. Furthermore, there is no parity in the two penalties, the one imposed by the rules of the game and the other imposed by Canon Law. The former penalizes the objective infringement of the rules of the game; the latter must consider the subjective culpability of the delinquent.

Article 4 — Loss of the Privilege of the Canon by General Law

According to canon 71 any privileges which are incorporated in the Code may be revoked by a subsequent general law. As has already been shown, privileges mentioned in the Code exist after the manner of laws, and therefore the general norms for the interpretation of laws are to be applied to them. From this it follows that canon 71, treating of the cessation of privileges in a wide sense, must be interpreted in the light of canon 22, which treats of the cessation of law. That is, the three ways of extrinsic cessation of law adduced by canon 22, namely, express revocation, direct contradiction, and complete revision of the former law, are to be understood as applying to canon 71.[49]

Since the privilege of the canon is a privilege in a wide sense,

49 Michiels, *Normae Generales*, II, 395.

it may, just as any other privilege mentioned in the Code, be revoked by a later general law which expressly repeals it, or is directly contrary to it, or which entirely readapts the matter of the privilege as it now exists. It should be noted, however, that no human legislator can divest the clerical state of its inherent dignity which in and of itself demands respect and reverence. The legislator, of course, could omit mention of the privilege in the general law, and could also omit or change the penalties which have been enacted to protect clerics from malicious real injury.

For the revocation of any privilege listed in the Code, however, express mention in the new law is not absolutely necessary. The mere incompatibility of the two general laws in this matter evinces the revocation of the privilege. But the incompatibility must be evident.[50] The reason for this is that the legislator is not presumed to be ignorant of any of the elements of the universal law.[51] If some future general law should state that only those who have received first tonsure, or who have made profession of vows in some religious institute, will henceforth enjoy the clerical privileges, then the privilege of the canon would certainly cease for novices. Such a general law would, of course, have to be promulgated and inserted in the Code according to the norm of the Motu proprio *Cum Iuris Canonici* issued by Benedict XV on September 15, 1917.[52]

The privileges listed in the Code, of which the privilege of the canon is one, can be revoked by certain clauses which are contained in a subsequent general law. According to the commonly accepted teaching, clauses such as *"non obstantibus privilegiis,"* or *"revocatis quibuscumque privilegiis,"* would not abrogate the privileges listed in the Code.[53] Privileges mentioned in

50 Roelker, *Principles of Privilege according to the Code of Canon Law*, p. 103.

51 Michiels, *op. cit.*, II, 395.

52 *AAS*, IX (1917), 483.

53 Ojetti, *Commentarium*, lib. I, ad can. 71, n. 1; Michiels, *Normae Generales*, II, 391; Beste, *Introductio in Codicem*, p. 122; Cicognani, *Canon Law*, p. 808. The same principles also prevailed in the old law. Cf. Schmalzgrueber, lib. V, tit. 33, n. 229.

the Code partake of the nature of laws and of privileges. In this connection Michiels asserts that in odious matters these privileges are to be considered as laws rather than as privileges.[54] Certainly their revocation would be something odious, and for that reason is not to be presumed. He concludes, then, that the clauses noted above would not be sufficient to abrogate privileges mentioned in the Code. But clauses such as "*non obstantibus quibuscumque privilegiis etiam expressa et specifica mentione dignis,*" or "*sub quacumque verborum forma conceptis*" would abrogate the privileges mentioned in the Code. The reason for this assertion is quite patent. Here the legislator is manifesting his will to revoke all privileges indiscriminately.

While it is possible for the privilege of the canon to cease in the manner just described it does not seem likely in view of the inherent nature of the privilege that it will ever cease in any such fashion. The clerical state is unalterably sacred. In consequence this state seems under any and all circumstances to demand its rightful protection.

54 Michiels, *loc. cit.*

CHAPTER VII

BENEFICIARIES OF THE PRIVILEGE OF THE CANON

Article 1 — Latin Clerics

A. *Preliminary Notions*

That the privilege of the canon is a real privilege which confers on its beneficiaries a favor has been established. The favor consists both of the obligation imposed on the faithful by law by which special reverence is due to clerics and religious in proportion to their divers grades in the hierarchy of orders or of jurisdiction, or in proportion to the office which they hold, and also of the prohibition under threat of sacrilege against the inflicting of any real (physical) injury upon clerics or religious.[1] It does not seem, as Goyeneche thinks, that the penalty established in canon 2343 against violators of the privilege of the canon is to be considered as an integrating element in the concept of the privilege.[2] His argument that the penal sanction is necessary for the integrity of the concept of the privilege of the canon inasmuch as the Code itself in its footnotes to canon 119 refers to canon 2343 has no officially authentic force at all. The footnotes were compiled by private authority and have no greater authority than the one who compiled them.

Canon 119, which asserts the personal immunity of clerics, makes no mention of the penal sanction which is contained in canon 2343, or vice versa. For this reason Cappello holds that there is no essential and necessary relationship between the two canons.[3] There is indeed some relationship between the two canons, since the purpose of the penal canon is to protect the

1 Teodori, "Privilegium Canonis—Consultationes"—*Apollinaris* (Romae, 1928 —), V (1932), 115.

2 "Consultationes" — *Commentarium pro Religiosis* (Romae, 1920 —), VII (1926), 188 (hereafter cited *CpR)*.

3 Cappello, "Praescriptum can. 2343, § 4, seu excommunicatio lata in percussores clericorum et religiosorum"—*Jus Pontificium* (Romae, 1921 —), V (1926), 31.

privilege, but it is not a relationship which is essential and necessary.[4]

Particular reverence would be due to the clerical state, and it would be a sacrilege to violate the person of a cleric independently of canon 2343. This has been proved historically, for special respect and reverence were due to the clerical state before Pope Innocent II introduced the canon of excommunication in the II General Council of the Lateran. Personal immunity from real (physical) injury must not be confused with the canonical sanction by which it is protected. Once equivocation and error arising from the confusion of these two ideas is removed, the interpretation of these two canons becomes more easily understood.

Canon 119, then, retains its force independently of canon 2343. Consequently the two canons are to be interpreted separately. Canon 119, to which canon 614[5] and canon 680[6] are also referred, is subject to a broad interpretation.[7] The broad interpretation is in order because one sees in the law a privilege granted by the legislator to those in the service of the Lord. Canon 2343, on the other hand, is a law which decrees a penalty, and for that reason is subject to a strict interpretation.[8] A strict interpretation clings to the text, and pays due regard to the mind of the legislator, but mitigates the rigor of the law as far as the law itself will permit.

The distinction between these two concepts is also important in that it lays the foundation for the distinction between those enjoying the privilege without the protection of any determinate

4 Cipollini, *De Censuris Latae Sententiae iuxta Codicem Iuris Canonici* (Taurini: Marietti, 1925), p. 172. Hereafter this work will be cited as *De Censuris.*

5 Canon 614 states: "Religiosi, etiam laici ac novitii, fruuntur clericorum privilegiis de quibus in can. 119-123."

6 Canon 680 which treats of societies of men and women living the common life without vows states: "Iidem, etiam laici, gaudent clericorum privilegiis, de quibus in can. 119-123, aliisque societati directe concessis, non autem privilegiis religiosorum sine speciali indulto."

7 Teodori, *loc. cit.*

8 Canon 19.

penal sanction and those enjoying the privilege protected by the sanction determined in canon 2343. This distinction is but mentioned in this place. A more detailed treatment of this question will be given in the section which treats of novices insofar as they enjoy the privilege of the canon.

B. Clerics Who Enjoy the Privilege

The privilege of the canon is enjoyed first of all by all clerics. Who are meant by clerics is evident from canon 108, § 1, namely, all those who have received at least first tonsure.[9] These men thereafter are assigned to the sacred ministry. Reception of first tonsure is sufficient for inscription in the clerical state and the consequent enjoyment of all clerical privileges. The use of the word *saltem* in canon 108 indicates clearly that one who has not received this sacred rite does not enjoy the privilege of the canon even though he wear the ecclesiastical dress. If clerics in first tonsure are protected, *a fortiori* those in higher orders, from the cleric in minor orders to the Pope himself, obviously share the protection afforded by this clerical privilege.

The penalties of excommunication, suspension, interdict, and deposition do not cause a cleric to lose the privilege of the canon. Respect is due to a cleric even though he has incurred one of these penalties, and anyone violating his personal immunity would be punished according to the norms of canon 2343.[10]

A cleric continues to enjoy the privilege of the canon along with the other clerical privileges as long as he has not lost it in one of the ways specified in the law. Canon 123 enumerates the various ways in which the clerical privileges can be lost, namely, through a reduction to the lay state, or through a perpetual denial of the right to wear the ecclesiastical dress and tonsure according to the norms of canon 213, § 1,[11] and 2304.[12] This

9 Canon 108, § 1: "Qui divinis ministeriis per primam saltem tonsuram mancipati sunt, clerici dicuntur."

10 Noldin-Schönegger, *De Censuris* (Oeniponte: Typis et Sumptibus Fel. Rauch, 1923), p. 82.

11 Canon 213, § 1: "Omnes qui e clericali statu ad laicalem legitime redacti aut regressi sunt, eo ipso amittunt officia, beneficia, iura ac privi-

enumeration does not seem to be explicitly exhaustive since no special mention is made in canon 123, which always includes reduction to the lay state with the consequent loss of ecclesiastical privileges.[13] Each of the various ways in which clerics can lose the clerical privileges will now be treated briefly.

C. *Loss of the Privilege*

1. Loss through Reduction to the Lay State:

Reduction to the lay state is the act which takes away the licit use of the power of Orders, deprives the cleric of his rights, privileges and juridic status, and makes the cleric equivalent to a layman.[14] The present study is not concerned with any of the other juridical effects of reduction to the lay state than the loss of the clerical privileges. Reduction to the lay state, no matter how it is effected, always entails the loss of the clerical privileges.

In the case of a cleric in major Orders, a reduction to the lay state is never effected *ipso facto*, for there is no mention in the law of any action the positing of which entails immediate laicization. Although a major cleric may be reduced to the lay state according to the norm of canon 211, § 1, it is important to observe that theologically this does not imply any change of status. Only in the eyes of the law and for certain legal effects such a cleric is considered a layman.[15]

legia clericalia et vetantur in habitu ecclesiastico incedere ac tonsuram deferre."

12 Canon 2304, § 1: "Si clericus depositus non det emendationis signa et praesertim si scandalum dare pergat monitusque non resipiscat, Ordinarius potest eum perpetuo privare iure deferendi habitum ecclesiasticum.

§ 2. "Haec privatio secumfert privationem privilegiorum clericalium et cessationem praescripti can. 2303, § 2."

13 Canon 2305. Cf. Findlay, *Canonical Norms Governing the Deposition and Degradation of Clerics*, The Catholic University of American Canon Law Studies, n. 130 (Washington, D. C.: The Catholic University of America Press, 1941), pp. 162 and 163.

14 Sipos, *Enchiridion Iuris Canonici* (Pécs: Ex Typographia "Haladás R. T.," 1926), p. 160.

15 Sweeney, *The Reduction of Clerics to the Lay State*, The Catholic

A cleric in major Orders may be reduced to the lay state in any of the three ways specified in the Code.[16] First, a cleric in major Orders may be reduced to the lay state by means of a rescript from the Holy See. Secondly, a cleric who has received a major Order through grave fear may be reduced to the lay state through a sentence of an ecclesiastical judge, provided that the cleric did not at least tacitly ratify his ordination through the exercise of the Order received with the intention of undertaking the obligations annexed to it.[17] Thirdly, a cleric in major Orders may be laicized by means of the penalty of degradation, which always includes reduction to the lay state.[18] An indirect method of reduction to the lay state results when a dispensation for marriage is granted to the major cleric in virtue of the faculties granted in canons 1043 and 1044. So, v. g., a deacon who is in danger of death might be dispensed from the impediment of sacred Orders according to the norms of these canons. This dispensation thus granted would in effect reduce the deacon to the lay state.[19]

Unlike major clerics, minor clerics may be reduced to the lay state through the placing of certain actions which are recognized by law as effecting an immediate reduction to the lay state.[20] The act which he places is not necessarily a delict, though it can be such, nor is it necessarily a prohibited act, though it may be such. But in any case the principle cause of the reduction is the will of the cleric, for he voluntarily places the act which effects his laicization.[21]

University of America Canon Law Studies, n. 223 (Washington, D. C.: The Catholic University of America Press, 1945), p. 121.

16 Canon 211, § 1: "Etsi sacra ordinatio, semel valide recepta, numquam irrita fiat, clericus tamen maior ad statum laicalem redigitur rescripto Sanctae Sedis, decreto vel sententia ad normam can. 214, demum poena degradationis."

17 Canon 214, § 1.

18 Canon 2305, § 1.

19 For a more detailed study on the reduction of major clerics to the lay state the reader is referred to Sweeney, *op. cit.*, pp. 121-165.

20 Canon 211, § 2.

21 Sweeney, *The Reduction of Clerics to the Lay State*, p. 46.

The first of these actions which effects a reduction to the lay state is marriage, or even an attempted marriage, on the part of the minor cleric.[22] The marriage need not necessarily be valid if it is to effect a reduction to the lay state with the consequent loss of the clerical privileges. But if a minor cleric should enter marriage through force or fear brought to bear on him, he would not fall from the clerical state.

Secondly, canon 136 prescribes for all clerics a distinct clerical dress which is to be determined by local customs. If a minor cleric has obstinately doffed the ecclesiastical dress and refused to wear the tonsure, he automatically loses his clerical status one month after he has been warned by his proper ordinary. Obstinate refusal is indicated by the fact that he has refused for one month to obey the injunction of the bishop to don it. After the lapse of the month he no longer has a right to the clerical privileges, for he has forfeited them through his fall from the clerical state.

Finally, a cleric is forbidden voluntarily and without the permission of his bishop to enlist with the armed forces.[23] Disobedience by a minor cleric to this prescription of the Code automatically causes him to fall from the clerical state. No sentence of the judge is necessary. A cleric is not permitted to volunteer without the necessary permission, even if it would mean a shorter term of service.[24]

A minor cleric may be reduced to the lay state not only in the various ways enumerated above, but he may also voluntarily return to it. The law in this case merely requires him to notify the local ordinary of his decision.[25] The local ordinary, too, for a just reason can issue a decree reducing a minor cleric to the lay state. He may do this if he prudently judges that the cleric cannot be promoted to higher Orders without disparagement to the clerical state.

22 Canon 132, § 2.

23 Canon 141.

24 Augustine, *A Commentary on Canon Law,* II, 94.

25 Canon 211, § 2.

2. Loss through Perpetual Denial of the Right to Wear the Ecclesiastical Dress:

Privation of the right to wear the clerical dress is, as it were, an approach to, and in milder manifestation an inceptive form of, degradation. Findlay states that the definition of this penalty in canon 2304 clearly indicates that it cannot legally exist apart from a previous deposition to which it brings added privation. For this reason he deems it more appropriate to designate this penalty of canon 2304 as aggravated deposition.[26]

Perpetual spoliation of the right to wear the ecclesiastical dress implies a privation of all the clerical privileges, and releases the ordinary from even the obligation in charity to provide the necessary support for an indigent cleric.[27] This penalty is to be inflicted on a deposed cleric who does not show any signs of amendment, and who persists in giving scandal and does not heed the warnings of his ordinary. For the protection of the clerical state there is no remedy but to take away the prerogatives of his rank.[28]

If and when a cleric is deposed he is deprived of all his ecclesiastical sources of income, even the benefice or pension which constituted his title of ordination. The ordinary is relieved from his obligation in justice to provide means for the support of the cleric inasmuch as the cleric has forfeited his right to demand sustenance. The legislator, however, imposes on the ordinary an obligation in charity to provide financial assistance to the cleric who is truly in need. But if the deposed cleric continues to give great scandal and does not amend in spite of warnings, then the ordinary may deprive him forever of the right to wear the ecclesiastical dress, which privation simultaneously brings with it the loss of all claim even to this charitable support.[29]

The Code also permits a temporary deprivation of the right to wear the ecclesiastical dress in cases of grave scandal. This

26 Findlay, *Canonical Norms Governing the Deposition and Degradation of Clerics*, p. 172.

27 Canon 2304, § 2.

28 Ayrinhac, *Penal Legislation in the New Code of Canon Law*, p. 126.

29 Findlay, *op. cit.*, pp. 167-171.

penalty may be inflicted when a cleric has spurned the bishop's warning to remove the cause of scandal and there is no possibility of removing the scandal in any other way.[30] The enjoyment of the clerical privileges in this case is suspended until the penalty is dispensed. But a cleric who has incurred this penalty does not lose his right to support since this penalty does not necessarily postulate as a prerequisite the infliction of the penalty of deposition. This latter penalty alone deprives the cleric of his right to sustenance.[31]

3. Loss through Degradation:

Before discussion is given to the loss of the clerical privileges through degradation it may be noted that the penalty of deposition does not inherently deprive a cleric of his clerical privileges.[32] The deposed cleric, therefore, remains a person consecrated to God by public authority and as such he is entitled to a proportionate degree of reverence. Deposition does, however, deprive a cleric of any dignities or offices which he has received, and as a consequence the deposed cleric has the status of a simple cleric. For that reason the excommunication which is incurred for a malicious assault upon a deposed cleric is always reserved to the ordinary regardless of what dignity or prelacy the cleric had obtained before he incurred the penalty of deposition.[33]

The penalty of degradation is the most severe vindicative penalty visited upon delinquent clerics. The effects of this penalty are deposition, perpetual privation of the right to wear the ecclesiastical dress and reduction to the lay state.[34] It has already been indicated that either one of these last two effects always entails loss of the clerical privileges.

30 Canon 2300.

31 Augustine, *A Commentary on Canon Law*, VIII, 257-258; Coronata, *Institutiones*, IV, 259.

32 Canon 2303, § 1.

33 Cf. canon 2343.

34 Canon 2305, § 1.

Article 2 — Oriental Clerics

The Code of Canon Law is concerned only with the discipline of the Latin Church, although it does in places make mention of the discipline of the Oriental Church.[35] The Code must be understood to bind Orientals only when it makes direct mention of them or when the Code-law binds Orientals in consequence of the very nature of the law *(ex ipsa rei natura)*. This latter exception leaves great margin for speculation as to when the nature of the law is such that it binds Orientals. The only question that is of concern in the present study is whether or not the privilege of the canon is of such a nature that it is enjoyed by Oriental clerics.

It can be said apodictically that all Oriental clerics enjoy the privilege of the canon.[36] This is true for the reason that the privilege of the canon protects rather the clerical state than the individual cleric. Hence the affiliation with a particular rite on the part of the individual cleric will not debar him from the enjoyment of this privilege. The inherent sacredness of the clerical state demands that it be respected without regard to the cleric's affiliation with any particular rite.

From time to time, however, the Holy See has expressly stated that priests belonging to one or the other of the various Oriental rites enjoy the privilege.[37] An examination of the latest available publication of sources for the codification of Oriental Canon Law, prepared by the Sacred Congregation for the Oriental Church, indicates that the privilege of the canon is specifically mentioned in the law of the Ruthenians,[38] the Ethiopians,[39] the Armenians[40] and Maronites.[41]

35 Cf. canon 1.

36 Cappello lists canon 119 as applying to Orientals.—*Summa Iuris Canonici* (3 vols., Romae: Apud Aedes Universitatis Gregorianae, Vol. I, 3. ed., 1938), I, 69.

37 Cf. *supra*, p. 42.

38 Sacra Congregazione Orientale, *Codificazione Canonica Orientale, Fonti* (Parte I, 16 vols., Parte II, 3 Serii, Roma: Tipografia Poliglotta Vaticana, 1930—), Serie I, Fascicolo XI, 69 (hereafter cited *Fonti)*.

39 *Fonti*, Serie I, Fascicolo V, 309.

40 *Fonti*, Serie I, Fascicolo VIII, 145.

41 *Fonti*, Serie III, Vol. II, 460.

Although all clerics of the various Oriental rites are immune from real (physical) injury, not all enjoy the privilege as protected by the sanction of a canonical censure.[42] Only one or the other of the various Oriental Churches has enacted legal measures entailing the excommunication for a violation. The lack of a penal sanction, however, does not in any way enervate the privilege, but rather conclusively proves that the sanction by way of a penalty is not a necessary and essential element of the privilege.

Article 3 — Religious

A. *Professed Religious*

Like the clerical state, the religious state is to be held in honor and respect by all in view of its divine origin and because of the great good, both spiritual and temporal, that has come to the Church as a result of it. Here again honor is to be given to the state itself, and the members of the state are to be held in esteem because of it.[43]

Religious hold a unique position in the Church. They do not belong to the clerical state, for they do not constitute part of the hierarchy. Fundamentally they belong to the lay state. Yet the Church has given them the obligations and privileges of clerics.[44] For this reason Coronata says they can be called clerics in a wide sense.[45]

A person is incorporated in the religious life by means of the profession of vows.[46] Only those who have made the profession of vows can be called religious in the strict sense of the word. Hence novices, postulants, and members of communities without vows cannot be called religious. By their profession religious are segregated from the laity, and obtain in a sense a public deputa-

42 Cappello, "Praescriptum can. 2343, § 4, seu excommunicatio lata in percussores clericorum et religiosorum" — *Jus Pontificium,* V (1926), 32.

43 Cf. canon 487. Beste, *Introductio in Codicem,* p. 306.

44 Canons 592; 614.

45 *Institutiones,* I, 197.

46 Canon 488, 7°.

tion for the enhancement of the divine worship.[47] For this reason they are considered as sacred persons. As such they must be respected. Any malicious, real (physical) injury perpetrated against them would constitute a personal sacrilege.[48] In other words, religious enjoy the privilege of the canon.[49]

This privilege is enjoyed by all religious, both men and women, whether they be in solemn or in simple vows. It makes no difference whether the religious belongs to a community of diocesan approval or to one of pontifical approval. The Code makes no distinction. Even lay religious, i.e., those religious who are not in the clerical state, enjoy this privilege. Among lay religious are comprised all nuns and sisters, as well as brothers in communities of men.

Religious enjoy the privilege of the canon along with the other clerical privileges as long as they belong to the religious state.[50] If a religious freely gives up the religious life he loses all claim to the privilege of the canon. Likewise a religious who is not a cleric loses all clerical privileges if he is dismissed from the community either by decree or by sentence of the proper superior, or for the performing of an action which implies an automatic dismissal.[51] The reason for this is patent. A religious enjoys the privilege of clerics because of his affliation with the religious life; but if the bond with the religious life is severed for any reason, he loses the privileges of clerics.

Apostates from a religious institute do not lose the clerical privileges which they enjoy as religious. Schaefer[52] and Riesner[53]

47 Schaefer (also Schäfer), *De Religiosis ad Normam Codicis Iuris Canonici* (3. ed., Romae: Typis Polyglottis Vaticanis, 1940), p. 38. Hereafter this work will be cited as *De Religiosis.*

48 Wernz-Vidal, *Ius Canonicum,* VIII *(Ius Poenale Ecclesiasticum).* Hereafter this volume will be cited as *Ius Poenale Ecclesiasticum.*

49 Canon 614.

50 Schaefer, *De Religiosis,* p. 776.

51 Canon 646.

52 *De Religiosis,* p. 776.

53 *Apostates and Fugitives from Religious Institutes,* The Catholic University of America Canon Law Studies, n. 168 (Washington, D. C.: The Catholic University of America Press, 1942), p. 91.

state that apostates from a religious institute forfeit the clerical privileges through their criminal act, although neither of the two writers offers any reason for their assertion. Their opinion on this point seems indefensible inasmuch as canon 2385, which enacts the penalties to be incurred by apostates from a religious community, indicates that the apostate is deprived of the privileges *suae religionis*.[54] The clerical privileges are enjoyed by religious not in virtue of their affliation with a particular community, but rather in virtue of their incorporation in the religious life. Hence in view of the strict interpretation which must be given to penal laws it must be maintained that the deprivation of privileges *suae religionis* of which mention is made in canon 2385, extends only to the privileges which have been granted to the religious institute of which the apostate is a member and not to the privileges which the apostate enjoys in common with all religious.[55]

Fugitives from religious institutes likewise continue to enjoy the privilege of the canon. Their legal ties with the religious are not considered broken, and hence there is no interruption in the enjoyment of any of the clerical privileges. In view of the strict interpretation which must be given to penal enactments, it must be maintained that fugitives from religious institutes continue to enjoy all the clerical privileges, among which the privilege of the canon is, of course, to be included.

In the preceding article of this dissertation it was noted that reduction to the lay state always entailed the loss of all clerical privileges. It is now to be observed that religious who are in major Orders can be reduced to the lay state in the same way as secular clerics in major Orders. The Code makes no special

54 Canon 2385: "Firmo praescriptio can. 646, religiosus apostata a religione, ipso iure incurrit in excommunicationem, proprio Superiori maiori vel, si religio sit laicalis aut non exempta, Ordinario loci in quo commoratur, reservatam, ab actibus legitimis ecclesiasticis est exclusus, *privilegiis* omnibus *suae religionis* privatus; et si redierit, perpetuo caret voce activa et passiva, ac praeterea aliis poenis pro gravitate culpae a Superioribus puniri debet ad normam constitutionum." The Italics have been inserted by the writer.

55 Cf. Augustine, *A Commentary on Canon Law,* VIII, 470.

provisions for the reduction of religious in sacred Orders to the lay state.

Religious minor clerics can also be reduced to the lay state in the same way as secular minor clerics. Therefore, what has been said about secular minor clerics can be understood as applicable to religious minor clerics. But it is necessary to consider the other ways as specified in the law by which religious minor clerics can be reduced to the lay state, for this reduction to the lay state also carries with it the loss of all the clerical privileges.

a. Dismissal of religious can be effected *ipso facto.* Religious who publicly apostatize from the Catholic faith, or who desert from their community with a person of the other sex, or who attempt or contract marriage, even a so-called civil marriage, are *ipso facto* dismissed from their religious institute. In these cases the law requires only that the major superior with his chapter or council make a declaration of the fact.[56]

Now, if a religious who is not a cleric is dismissed for one of these reasons there is no doubt that he loses the clerical privileges. The reason is that the religious is legally considered to have forfeited the religious life. It is not clear, however, whether a religious minor cleric who is *ipso facto* dismissed is reduced to the lay state. Most of the authors maintain that the dismissal includes the reduction to the lay state.[57]

Sweeney, however, holds, although hesitatingly, that the dismissal mentioned in canon 646 does not include reduction to the lay state.[58] He argues from the fact that canon 648 indicates that religious minor clerics who are dismissed *"ad normam can. 647"* are by that very fact reduced to the lay state.[59] Sweeney

56 Canon 646.

57 Coronata, *Institutiones,* I, 871; Vermeersch-Creusen, *Epitome,* I, n. 821; O'Neill, *The Dismissal of Religious in Temporary Vows,* The Catholic University of America Canon Law Studies, n. 166 (Washington, D. C.: The Catholic University of America Press, 1942), p. 126.

58 *The Reduction of Clerics to the Lay State,* p. 75.

59 Canon 648: "Religiosus dimissus ad normam can. 647 ipso facto solvitur ab omnibus votis religiosis, salvis oneribus ordini maiori adnexis, si sit in sacris, et firmo praescripto can. 641, § 1; 642; clericus autem in minoribus ordinibus constitutus eo ipso redactus est in statum laicalem."

maintains that it would be difficult, if not impossible, to bring forward a reason for the insertion in canon 648 of the phrase *"ad normam can. 647"* if the minor clerics who have been dismissed in accordance with the ruling of canon 646 are also contemplated in canon 648. This seems to be the better opinion in view of the fact that the Code in no way indicates that the dismissal according to canon 646 implies a reduction to the lay state. Practically this means that a religious minor cleric who is automatically dismissed from a religious institute according to the norm of canon 646 continues to possess the clerical privileges.

b. The second way in which a religious minor cleric can be reduced to the lay state is by means of a dismissal according to the norm of canon 647. This canon states that the supreme moderator of a religious institute or the abbot of an independent monastery, each with the consent of his respective council, obtained by secret ballot, may dismiss one who is professed in temporary vows in an Order or in a Congregation of pontifical approval. In a Congregation of diocesan approval the local ordinary may dismiss one who is in temporary vows.

One of the juridic effects of dismissal according to these norms is that a religious minor cleric is *ipso facto* reduced to the lay state.[60] Hence a religious minor cleric so dismissed is automatically deprived of the privilege of the canon.[61]

c. Canon 669, § 2, indicates that a religious minor cleric in perpetual vows who has been dismissed from his religious institute is by that very fact reduced to the lay state. Therefore, the dismissal of such a cleric, no matter how effected, would cause the cleric to be reduced to the lay state. In accordance with canon 123 and 213, § 1, the clerical privileges would be lost. It is true that a religious minor cleric in perpetual vows continues to be a religious until he obtains a dispensation from the vows; but it does not seem that he would still retain the clerical privileges until he ceases to be a religious. Canon 123 together with canon 213, § 1, indicates that *all* who are reduced to the lay state lose the clerical privileges. Most of the authors support this

60 Canon 648.

61 Canon 123.

statement and indicate that such a cleric loses the privileges both as a cleric and as a religious.[62]

d. Finally, a religious cleric in minor orders is to be dismissed from the clerical state if his profession was declared null because of intrigue perpetrated by him. Again, reduction to the lay state in this instance means loss of the clerical privileges.[63]

B. Novices

Novices make no profession of public vows, yet in favorable matters the law makes them equivalent to religious. So, e. g., they share in all the privileges and spiritual favors granted to their community, they are exempt from the jurisdiction of the local ordinary, etc.[64] Likewise in the matter of the clerical privileges they are put on a par with professed religious. Hence as long as they are novices they enjoy the privilege of personal immunity, and any violation of the privilege would constitute a sacrilege.[65]

Although the Code in crystal-clear words grants them the privilege of the canon, there has been a great deal of controversy whether or not they enjoy it as protected by the canonical sanction of the censure of excommunication. The question is whether or not a person who maliciously strikes a novice falls under the excommunication enacted in canon 2343, § 4.[66] That canon enacts

62 Schaefer, *De Religiosis*, p. 1023; Cocchi, *Commentarium*, lib. II, Pars II, n. 157; Fanfani, *De Iure Religiosorum* (2. ed., Taurini-Romae: Marietti, 1925), p. 367; Sweeney, *The Reduction of Clerics to the Lay State*, p. 87. O'Leary, however, seems to imply that a minor cleric, in spite of his reduction to the lay state, retains the clerical privileges for the reason that he is still a religious. — *Religious Dismissed after Perpetual Profession*, The Catholic University of America Canon Law Studies, n. 184 (Washington, D. C.: The Catholic University of America Press, 1943), p. 95.

63 Canon 2387.

64 Canon 567, § 1; 615, etc.

65 Cf. canons 119 and 614. Piscetta-Gennaro, *Elementa Theologiae Moralis* (7 vols., Vol. IV, 2. ed., Torino: Società Editrice Internazionale, 1929), IV, 288.

66 In this discussion whatever is said concerning novices must also be applied to quasi-religious, since they are not religious as defined in canon 488, 7°. Some authors who discuss this point make no reference to the

an excommunication to be incurred *ipso facto* by those who lay violent hands *"in personam aliorum clericorum*[47] *vel utriusque sexus religiosorum."* Authors are divided in their opinions concerning the interpretation of the word *religiosorum.* The subject of the controversy is whether this term is to be understood as it is defined in canon 488, 7°, or whether it is used in canon 2343, § 4, in a broader sense, so that novices become included under its scope.

At the very outset of this discussion it must be admitted that it is the common opinion of the authors that novices as well as those who are regarded *ad instar religiosorum* are included under the term *religiosorum* of canon 2343, § 4.[68] Most of the authors do not give very convincing reasons for their opinion, if they give any. Of all the authors who support this opinion Goyeneche has advanced the most persuasive arguments. For that reason the development of his view will be considered briefly.

Goyeneche holds that the penal sanction is necessary for a complete concept of the privilege of the canon. For him the privilege consists of two elements, i. e., of the obligation to show

quasi-religious, but their arguments are applicable to the quasi-religious as well as to novices.

67 The words *"aliorum clericorum"* have reference to all clerics not mentioned in the preceding paragraphs of the canon. It includes all clerics who do not belong to the rank of Cardinals, of papal legates, or at least of titular bishops.

68 Noldin-Schönegger, *De Censuris,* p. 82; Mothon, *Institutions Canoniques a l'usage des Curies Episcopales, du Clergé Paroissial, et des Familles Religieuses* (3 vols., Brugis: Desclée, De Brouwer, 1922-1924), II, 752; Chelodi, *Ius Poenale et Ordo Procedendi in Iudiciis Criminalibus iuxta Codicem Iuris Canonici* (Tridenti: Libr. Edit. Tridentum, 1925 [1920!]), p. 96; Blat, *Commentarium Textus Codicis Iuris Canonici* (5 vols. in 6, Romae: Ex Typographia Pontificia in Instituto Pii IX, 1919-1927), II, 699 (hereinafter cited *Commentarium); Cavigioli, De Censuris Latae Sententiae quae in Codice Iuris Canonici Continentur Commentariolum* (Torino: Libraria Editrice Internazionale, 1919), p. 131 (hereinafter cited *De Censuris);* Wernz-Vidal, *Ius Poenale Ecclesiasticum,* p. 494; Vermeersch-Creusen, *Epitome,* III, n. 542; Cocchi, *Commentarium,* VIII, 285-286: Goyeneche, "Consultationes"—*CpR,* VII (1926), 186-190; Pistocchi, *I Canoni Penali del Codice Ecclesiastico* (Torino-Roma: Marietti, 1925), p. 142; et alii.

reverence to clerics, and of the penal sanction which punishes violations. From this he argues that all religious enjoy the privilege integrally, i. e., they are immune from real injury, and any violation is punishable with an excommunication to be incurred *ipso facto.* He claims that novices enjoy the privilege of the canon in the same way as professed religious, i. e., integrally. Therefore, they too enjoy the privilege as protected by means of the penal sanction. Secondly, he appeals to the old law, stating that no change has been introduced by the Code, and under the old law novices were protected by means of the penalty of excommunication which was in store for persons who maliciously assaulted them.[69] The Code has reproduced the penal enactments for violations of the privilege of the canon as they were contained in the Constitution *Apostolicae Sedis* of October 12, 1869, except that in the Code the word *monachos* has been changed to *religiosorum.*[70] Canon 2343 restates the old law, and therefore, according to canon 6, 2° and 3°, it is to be interpreted in the light of the old law.

Goyeneche denies application of the principles *"in poenis benignior est interpretatio facienda"* and *"non licet poenam de persona ad personam vel de casu ad casum producere quamvis par adsit ratio, imo gravior."*[71] These principles, so he contends, do not enter into the question because the subject-matter under the old law and the new law is identical, although new terminology is used. To deny that malicious strikers of novices incur excommunication would mean for Goyeneche a complete change in the concept of the privilege of the canon. As a final argument he appeals to extrinsic authority.[72]

Cipollini, who also subscribes to this opinion, adds another reason which may well be considered.[73] He admits that the cen-

69 C. 21, *de sententia excommunicationis, suspensionis et interdicti,* V, 11, in VI°.

70 *Fontes,* n. 552. For a consideration of the penalty as contained in the Constitution *Apostolicae Sedis* cf. *supra* pp. 43-45.

71 Canon 2219.

72 Goyeneche cites most of the authors which have been cited above in a footnote as supporting this opinion.

73 *De Censuris,* p. 172.

sure itself is something odious, but the cause for which the censure has been enacted is a favorable matter. The purpose of the penalty is to protect the status and the dignity of persons who are dedicated to the service of God. This purpose is to be attained also in the case of novices. As in other favorable matters, here, too, novices are put on a par with professed religious.

Although most of the commentators on this point follow this opinion, and although it is admitted to be the common opinion, nonetheless the arguments advanced in support of it do not seem to be sufficiently compelling. For this reason it seems best to adopt the opinion of Cappello,[74] who is the foremost supporter of the opinion which denies that malicious strikers of novices and of those living in communities without vows incur the excommunication. He calls his opinion certain both theoretically and practically. It seems best to adopt this opinion because of the intrinsic argumentation with which it is supported.

Religious are defined by the Code as those who have taken vows in some religious community.[75] Admittedly, novices can be said to be beginning a religious life, but they cannot be called religious in a legal sense, for they have not as yet taken vows. From the clear and express terminology of the Code neither novices nor those living in common without vows can be called religious. That the term "religious" is always to be understood in the same sense is clear from canon 488, which indicates without exception that in the canons which are to follow, religious are those who take vows in some religious institute.[76] If it is

74 "Praescriptum can. 2343, § 4 seu excommunicatio lata in percussores clericorum et religiosorum" — *Jus Pontificium,* V (1926), 29-33. The following also hold this opinion: De Meester, *Juris Canonici et Juris Canonico-Civilis Compendium* (ed. nova, 3 vols. in 4, Brugis: Desclée, De Brouwer, 1921-1928), IV, 254; Pighi, *Censurae Sententiae Latae et Irregularitates quas habet "Codex Iuris Canonici"* (7. ed., Verona: Cinquetti, 1922), n. 102; Teodori, "Privilegium Canonis — Consultationes" — *Apollinaris,* V (1932), 112-116; Piscetta-Gennaro, *Elementa Theologiae Moralis,* IV, 288-289.

75 Canon 488, 7°.

76 "In canonibus qui sequuntur, veniunt nomine: . . . Religiosorum, qui vota nuncuparunt in aliqua religione."

said that novices and members of communities leading the common life without vows are included under the term *religiosorum* of canon 2343, § 4, one would be obliged to conclude that the term is not used uniformly throughout the Code. Canon 2343, § 4, would have to be an exception to the general principle of canon 488, and this in turn would imply a contradiction in the law.

If novices and those living in communities without vows were to be included in canon 2343, § 4, then specific mention of them would have to be made. This is in strict accord with the principle that laws which determine penalties are subject to a strict interpretation.[77] This is also in harmony with the provision of canon 2219, § 1, which states that in penalties the more favorable interpretation is to be applied.

The reasons alleged by the opponents of this opinion are all answerable. Canon 119 gives a genuine concept of the personal immunity of clerics, and makes no reference to the penal canon. Personal immunity from real injury implies reverence for the clerical or the religious state, and the guilt of sacrilege for any violations of that immunity. These two ideas are separable from and independent of the punishment enacted against violators. Hence, if the penal canon were necessary for an integral concept of the privilege, then the canon indicating the privilege would have to mention the penal canon. It is always logical to conclude that a canon in and of itself contains a complete and integral concept unless there is reference in the canon to some other canon. That the notion of reverence for clerics and for religious can be understood without reference to the sanction of excommunication is proved from the fact that Orientals enjoy the privilege, although most of the Oriental rites have no penalty for violations.[78] Furthermore, if the penalty is an essential and constitutive part of the concept of the privilege of the canon, then any change in the penalty would necessarily imply an essential change in the privilege of the canon. But it does not seem reasonable to make this implication.

77 Canon 19.

78 Cf. *supra*, p. 73.

To exclude novices from canon 2343, § 4, does not imply a change in the concept of the privilege. The Code has merely determined who are considered as religious in the new law. This was not clear in the old law.[79] It must be admitted that the new law must be interpreted in the light of the old law if the new law is identical with the old.[80] But here the new law is not related *exactly* as in the old law. First of all, the Code makes use of the word *religiosorum* in place of the word *monachos* as found in the old law. Secondly, the reservation of the penalty was changed. Formerly this was a penalty reserved to the Pope for absolution, and now the ordinary can absolve. At most, therefore, it can be said that the new law only partially restates the old law. Consequently it is to be interpreted according to the interpretations of the old law only insofar as it agrees.

It is making a gratuitous statement to assert that all novices enjoy the privilege in the same way as professed religious, i. e., as protected by the sanction of the censure. Anyone making this assertion must prove conclusively that the term "religious" is used in canon 2343, § 4, in a sense entirely different than in any other part of the Code. The present writer thinks, although with some hesitancy, that it would take an extensive interpretation to include novices and members of communities without vows under the terms of the canon in question.

It will be recalled that Goyeneche appealed to authority in support of his opinion. But it must also be remembered that the authority of authors is not established as a norm of interpretation of the law of the Code unless the law of the Code is identical with the old law. The Code itself indicates that ecclesiastical laws must be interpreted according to the proper meaning of the terms of the law considered in their text and context.[81] Nothing in the text or context of canon 2343, § 4, indicates that the term *religiosorum* is to be understood in any other sense than as defined in canon 488.

79 Cappello, *De Censuris iuxta Codicem Iuris Canonici* (2. ed., Taurinorum Augustae: Marietti, 1925), p. 333 (hereafter cited *De Censuris).*

80 Canon 6, 2° and 3°.

81 Canon 18.

Finally, the argument advanced by Cipollini, who holds that novices enjoy the privilege of the canon *sub censura* inasmuch as the cause for which the censure has been passed is a favorable matter, can be refuted. It seems that Cipollini is arguing from the purpose of the law before he considers the clear words of the text. An interpretation based on the purpose of the law is permitted only in the case of doubt. But there does not seem to be any doubt as to the meaning and usage of the term "religious" in this canon 2343, for the definition of the term can be found in the Code itself.

For all these reasons, then, the opinion of Cappello seems to be the better of the two. In actual practice it does not seem possible to hold that the malicious strikers of novices, or of members of communities without vows, incur excommunication, for it must be admitted that there is here a *dubium iuris.* The doubt here arises not so much from the wording of the law as from the extrinsic authority which supports the contrary opinion. But once a *dubium iuris* is admitted, the excommunication cannot be urged.[82]

C. *Postulants*

Before admission to the novitiate all women in communities which take perpetual vows and all lay brothers who are in communities whose members take solemn vows must make a postulancy for at least six months. During that period the postulants wear a distinctive religious habit and lead a kind of religious life under the immediate supervision of religious superiors.[83] They may even be said to belong to the religious family. The life of postulants so closely approximates the life of religious that in monasteries of nuns the postulants are subject to the laws of the cloister during their postulancy.

For these reasons some authors extend to postulants the privilege of the canon.[84] They also argue that this is a favorable

82 Canon 15.

83 Canons 539 to 541.

84 Fanfani, *De Iuris Religiosorum,* p. 230; Coronata, *Institutiones,* I, 213. Coronata says they enjoy it *sub censura.*

law and is subject to a broad interpretation. In some cases the Code has extended to them the rights of novices.[85]

But since the Code itself has not expressly extended this privilege to postulants, the majority of the authors holds that they do not enjoy its protection.[86] Postulants are not mentioned in canon 614, and that is equivalent to exclusion. It is true that they belong to a religious family under the immediate direction of superiors, but they have no claim to any of the clerical privileges because of their affiliation with a religious family. This statement seems to be corroborated from the tenor of a decision of the Pontifical Commission for the Interpretation of the Code. The Commission on July 20, 1929, decided that the provisions of canon 1221 do not apply to postulants.[87] Canon 1221 states that professed religious and novices after their demise may be transferred for burial to the church or oratory of their house, or to a church or oratory belonging to the religious institute, unless the novices have chosen another church for burial. After this response it no longer seems possible to hold as a general principle that postulants enjoy all the privileges and spiritual favors granted to the community. The same can be said concerning the clerical privileges.[88]

ARTICLE 4 — QUASI-RELIGIOUS

The privilege of the canon is also enjoyed by persons who belong to societies, whether of men or of women, whose members imitate the manner of life of religious, by living in community under the government of ecclesiastical superiors according to approved constitutions, but without the usual three vows.[89] Members of these societies are not religious in the strict sense of the word, for they do not take vows in their communities.

85 Cf., e.g., canons 1312, § 1; 1313, 2°.

86 Ayrinhac, *Penal Legislation in the New Code of Canon Law,* p. 224; Beste, *Introductio in Codicem,* p. 417; Schaefer, *De Religiosis,* pp. 454 and 455; Cappello, *De Censuris,* p. 330; Augustine, *A Commentary on Canon Law,* VIII, 379; Cavigioli, *De Censuris,* p. 130; et alii.

87 *AAS,* XXI (1929), 573.

88 Schaefer, *De Religiosis,* p. 455.

89 Canon 680.

The individual members may take private vows, an oath of obedience, or a promise of stability, but they cannot be called religious. Yet all members of these communities, lay as well as clerical, enjoy the privilege of the canon.

The Code makes no provision for a novitiate for these quasi-religious, and consequently this matter is left entirely up to the Constitutions.[90] The only provision made in this regard by the Code is that if there is a novitiate, then the regulations for valid and licit admission prescribed by the Code must be observed.[91] But the question to be resolved here is whether or not novices in any of these communities without vows which have a novitiate enjoy the privilege of the canon.

Surely novices in these communities are considered in the same relation to their community as novices in strictly so-called religious institutes. The novitiate is a probationary period for the candidate during which the candidate is preparing for profession. Hence it seems that novices in communities without vows enjoy the privilege at least by the very force of analogy. Furthermore, since the privilege in favorable matters is subject to a broad interpretation, it can be extended to include these novices.[92]

In those societies which do not have a novitiate the enjoyment of the privilege begins when the candidate is formally admitted into the ranks of the society. This follows from the fact that canon 680 indicates that the *members* of communities without vows enjoy the clerical privilege.

At this point mention can also be made of hermits. The Code does not give them legal recognition. Consequently they do not enjoy the clerical privileges. But if they have grouped themselves together and live in common and have received the habit from competent authority they can be considered quasi-religious.

90 Wernz-Vidal, *Ius Canonicum*, III (Romae: Universitas Gregoriana, 1933), 409.

91 Canon 677.

92 Berutti, *Institutiones Iuris Canonici* (6 vols., Vol. III, Taurini-Romae: Marietti, 1936), III, 371; Augustine, *A Commentary on Canon Law*, VIII, 379.

As such they would enjoy the clerical privileges.[93] Those hermits, however, who live for themselves, even though they have the approval of ecclesiastical authority and wear the religious habit, have no claim to the privilege of the canon or any of the other clerical privileges.

What has been said about hermits can be applied also to members of Third Orders. If they lead a common life under the government of superiors with approved constitutions, but without being bound by vows, they enjoy the privilege of the canon.[94]

In accordance with the opinion adopted in the preceding article of this dissertation, it is here to be noted that none of those just mentioned as enjoying the privilege of the canon enjoy it *sub censura*. Neither quasi-religious, nor hermits, nor tertiaries can be considered religious as defined in canon 488, 7°, and for that reason they are not included under the term *"religiosorum"* of canon 2343, § 4.

It may be objected that the privilege of the canon is of no advantage to those who do not enjoy it as protected by means of the censure of excommunication. But in answer to this objection it can be observed that reverence and respect are due to all those who enjoy the privilege. Furthermore, any violation of the privilege constitutes a sacrilege.[95] If it is a delict, there must be some canonical penalty, at least indeterminate, established in the law.[96] If, therefore, there is a violation of the privilege of the canon by means of a malicious injury inflicted on one who enjoys the privilege, but who does not enjoy it *sub censura*, it seems to the present writer that this delict is punishable according to the norm of canon 2325. This canon gives the ordinary power to punish, in proportion to the gravity of the guilt, those who perpetrate a sacrilegious act. The ordinary can use this power only in cases wherein the law has not determined a specific penalty for certain acts of sacrilege. In the case in question there is no penalty determined. Hence, it seems that the application of this canon is fully warranted.

93 Augustine, *A Commentary on Canon Law,* II, 59; Ayrinhac, *Penal Legislation in the New Code of Canon Law,* p. 224.

94 Cappello, *De Censuris,* p. 330.

95 Canon 119.

96 Canon 2195, § 1.

CHAPTER VIII

THE EXCOMMUNICATION INVOKED AGAINST VIOLATORS

Article 1 — Relationship of the Present Law to the Old

Canon 2343. — §1 Qui violentas manus in personam Romani Pontificis iniecerit:

1° Excommunicationem contrahit latae sententiae Sedi Apostolicae specialissimo modo reservatam; et est ipso facto vitandus;

§ 2. Qui in personam S. R. E. Cardinalis vel Legati Romani Pontificis:

1° In excommunicationem incurrit latae sententiae Sedi Apostolicae speciali modo reservatam;

§ 3. Qui in personam Patriarchae, Archiepiscopi, Episcopi etiam titularis tantum, incurrit in excommunicationem latae sententiae Sedi Apostolicae speciali modo reservatam.

§ 4. Qui in personam aliorum clericorum vel utriusque sexus religiosorum, subiaceat ipso facto excommunicationi Ordinario proprio reservatae, . . .

The enacted excommunication as incurred by those who maliciously strike clerics has existed in the universal Church law since 1139, and during the centuries that have elapsed since then many Popes have issued decrees relative to this penalty. This excommunication has also been treated rather extensively by canonists during these years. With eight hundred years of development it can hardly be gainsaid that this particular penalty was well developed at the time of its insertion into the present Code of Canon Law. All this past development can be used to great advantage in explaining and interpreting the present law.

If the Code restates the old law in its entirety, then the interpretations as given by approved authors of the old law are to be followed. If, however, a particular canon agrees only in part with the old law, then it must be interpreted in accordance with the old law only insofar as the new law agrees with the old.[1] Accordingly, it is now to be determined to what extent the present law agrees with the old. To this end a brief comparison will be drawn between the present law and the old for the sake of delineating the differences.

The penal law of censures which prevailed at the time of the publication of the Code was the Constitution *Apostolicae Sedis* of Pius IX (1846-1878).[2] Hence it is sufficient to make a comparison between the present canon enacting the excommunication with the canon enacted in that Constitution. With the exception of the differences to be pointed out the legislation is identical.

In the old law there was no special censure enacted for the case which implied a personal attack upon the Supreme Pontiff. Excommunications reserved *specialissimo modo* were unknown in the old law. Secondly, the famous phrase *"suadente diabolo"* has been omitted by the new law, but this omission by the legislator implies no limitation of the extent of this law, since that phrase postulated nothing more than a gravely sinful action, which demand is now incorporated in the Code itself simply in view of the norms enacted in the law itself.[3] Thirdly, as has already been mentioned, the Code has changed the word *monachos* to *religiosorum* in accordance with the new terminology adopted by the Code.

Fourthly, under the pre-Code law the excommunication incurred for the malicious striking of a cleric or of a monk was reserved in a special way to the Pope. In the new law this crime is reserved for absolution to the proper Ordinary. Fifthly, the old law specifically mentioned which actions involved the incurring of excommunication when Cardinals, patriarchs, archbishops, bishops, apostolic delegates and nuncios of the Holy See

1 Canon 6, 2° and 3°.

2 *Fontes*, n. 552. Cf. *supra*, pp. 43-45.

3 Sole, *De Delictis et Poenis* (Romae: Pustet, 1920), p. 296. Even in his own day Suarez (†1617) remarked that this traditional expression simply implied that the excommunication was not incurred unless the *percussio* constituted a grave sin. — *De Censuris in Communi*, disp. XXII, sect. I, n. 5 *(Omnia Opera*, Vol. XXIII [Parisiis, 1866], 545).

were the passive subjects of the injury. This minute specification of the actions which gave rise to the excommunication is omitted in the new law, but all of these actions are implied in the expression *violentas manus iniecerit.*

Finally, the Constitution *Apostolicae Sedis* made special mention of the *mandantes, vel rata habentes, seu praestantes in eis auxilium, consilium vel favorem,* in connection with the censure incurred for the laying of violent hands on the members of the hierarchy. With the exception of the *rata habentes* these are all governed by the principles enunciated in canon 2209. In the new law the *rata habentes* are not subject to the excommunication.

It is again emphasized that this comparison covers only the differences in the statement of the law as it prevailed either immediately prior to the enactment of the Code or immediately subsequent thereto. Furthermore, the comparison has reference only to the censure of excommunication.

In the place where the two laws differ the canon in the new law must be interpreted according to the meaning of the words employed. But for the most part the new law agrees with the old, and hence the authority of approved authors in the old law can be used to interpret the present canon.

Article 2 — Persons Liable to the Penalty

The active subject of real injury against clerics or religious can be any baptized person, man or woman, who is capable of committing grave sin. The clergy as well as laity can be guilty of this crime. Non-Catholics, too, can be guilty of and punished for laying violent hands on the person of clerics or religious.

Canon 2343, which makes mention of the excommunication to be incurred for the sacrilegious maltreatment of clerics or of religious, is concerned only with the one who actually and physically performs the act.[4] No mention is made of those at whose command the crime is committed nor of co-operators. In this regard the provisions of canon 2209, which deals with co-opera-

[4] "Qui violentas manus . . . iniecerit."

tion in delinquencies, must be applied. Conspirators, i. e., those who by means of mutual counsel to commit a crime concur physically or actually in its perpetration are equally responsible with the criminal, unless circumstances increase or diminish their culpability. Hence the *percussores clericorum*, if they concur in the same criminal act, are all guilty, even though only one may strike the blow.[5]

In a similar manner the principals or participators in a crime are equally guilty with the actual culprit, if their influence was so efficacious that the deed would not have been perpetrated without it. In this group are included the *mandans* or principal author of the crime, the instigators and the aiders and abettors *(concurrentes)* in whatsoever form. All these are subject to the excommunication, provided that the guilt is not diminished in one or the other of them through ignorance of the law, or for any other reason of similar import.[6] It will help to clarify these principles by means of a few practical examples. If an employer should order one of his employees to shoot a priest, both the employer and employee would incur the same penalty. The employer in this case is the *mandans*. An instigator would be, v. g., a layman who invites others to help him engage in fisticuffs with his pastor because of some disagreement. All those engaging in the fight would be excommunicated. If in this fight the pastor was gaining the upper hand, and thereupon someone furnished the layman with a pistol to shoot the pastor, then the one furnishing the gun would be concurring in the crime. He too would fall under the excommunication as an abettor.

When consideration was being given to the possibility of renouncing the clerical privileges, it was pointed out that a cleric or a religious may never submit himself to physical injury which

5 Raus, *Institutiones Canonicae* (2. ed., Lugduni-Parisiis: Typis Emmanuelis Vitte, 1931), p. 714; Ferreres, *Institutiones Canonicae*, I, 99; Cappello, *De Censuris* (1925 edition), pp. 252 and 333. In his 1919 edition (p. 63) Cappello had taught that co-operators and *mandantes* in connection with this crime did not fall under the censure. He there argued from the fact that there was no mention of them in canon 2343.

6 Canon 2209, § 3.

is degrading to the clerical state.[7] If, however, a cleric should submit himself to such an injury, e. g., as a means of satisfaction for an injury inflicted by the cleric, the person so inflicting the injury is not immune from the ecclesiastical penalty. At first blush this seems contradictory to the principle: *"Scienti et consentienti non fit iniuria neque dolus."* [8] This principle, however, has no application in the present case, for no cleric is at liberty to alienate prerogatives granted to the clerical state.[9]

There has also been discussed the question whether or not the excommunication is incurred by a cleric who with evil intention would strike himself.[10] No reference is here made to clerics who, moved by a spirit of penance, submit themselves to the discipline. The point in question is concerned only with a cleric who, prompted by evil intention, mutilates, injures, or even kills himself. But these cases do not seem to be comprehended under canon 2343, for this law must be understood as referring to others who lay violent hands on a cleric or a religious, and not to those in whose favor the law has been made.[11] This is corroborated by the fact that canon 2350, § 2, deals with those who lay hands on themselves.[12] Clerics who are guilty of attempted suicide or self-destruction are forbidden as Catholics to perform any legally authorized ecclesiastical acts, and as clerics they must be suspended for a period to be fixed by the ordinary, and must be removed from any benefice or office connected with the care of souls, both in the internal and external forum. This crime presupposes malice; therefore, if the incident was due to accident or to insanity, even temporary, the penalties would not be in-

7 *Supra,* pp. 58-61.

8 Reg. 27, R. J., in VI°.

9 C. 36, X, *de sententia excommunicationis,* V, 39.

10 Noldin-Schönegger, *De Censuris,* p. 83.

11 Cipollini, *De Censuris,* p. 121; cf. Schmalzgrueber, lib. V, tit. 39, n. 225.

12 Canon 2350, § 2: "Qui in seipsos manus intulerint, si quidem mors secuta sit, sepultura ecclesiastica priventur ad normam can. 1240, § 1, n. 3; secus, arceantur ab actibus legitimis ecclesiasticis et, si sint clerici, suspendantur ad tempus ad Ordinario definiendum, et a beneficiis aut officiis curam animarum interni vel externi fori adnexam habentibus removeantur."

curred.[13] Since these penalties are specifically established for those clerics who maliciously lay violent hands on themselves, it is safe to conclude that such clerics are not subject to the penalties of canon 2343 for this crime.

Those also are liable to excommunication who by law or grave fear are forced to inflict real injury on clerics or on religious, if in the act there is manifested a contempt of faith or of ecclesiastical authority, or if there is any public harm accruing to souls as a result of it.[14] If a person motivated by grave fear strikes a cleric or a religious, and in his act there is no sign of contempt of faith or of ecclesiastical authority and his action likewise causes no public harm to souls, he does not incur the excommunication. In this connection one can imagine the case of a priest who is incarcerated in a country where Catholics are persecuted. If the guard of the jail inflicts any injuries and insults on the priest because of his own hatred for Catholicism, even though he were under the necessity of doing so because of a command from higher authority, he would still incur the excommunication. If the guard executes orders which are motivated through a contempt of faith but he does not advert to this motivation through inculpable ignorance, his act may not be sinful and accordingly provides no basis for the incurring of the censure.[15]

As a general rule every baptized person who has the use of reason and is capable of malice is potentially a proper passive subject of the censures established in the law of the Code. However, it is indicated by the legislator that, unless they receive express mention in the penal law, Cardinals do not incur the penalties enacted in the Code.[16] Since it is not mentioned in canon 2343 that Cardinals are subject to the penalties enacted therein, they are not liable to any of its penal sanctions. This immunity from penal law, however, applies only to the Cardinals

13 Ayrinhac, *Penal Legislation in the New Code of Canon Law*, p. 242.

14 Cf. canon 2205, § 3.

15 Teodori, "Privilegium Canonis — Consultationes" — *Apollinaris*, V (1932), 116.

16 Canon 2227, § 2.

who have been created and nominated by the Roman Pontiff in a consistory.[17] If the Roman Pontiff announces in consistory the creation of a Cardinal, but reserves the name to himself, the person thus promoted does not in the meantime enjoy any of the rights and privileges of Cardinals. Furthermore, Cardinals enjoy this exemption from penal law only as long as they are Cardinals.[18] If for any reason they lose the cardinalate, they lose with it also their exemption from the penal law, and they then become liable to the penalties of canon 2343.

Consideration may here be given to the conceivable, though not at all likely, case of a Cardinal co-operating with others in inflicting malicious physical injury on another cleric. Even though the action itself were done by the Cardinal, any accomplices who themselves are not Cardinals are liable to the penalties enacted in canon 2343 according to the norm of canons 2209 and 2231. The Cardinal alone is exempt from the penal law, but not the others.

The excommunication for a violation of the privilege of the canon can be incurred even by the rulers of nations, and also by their offspring or by their successors in the government. Only the Roman Pontiff, however, can issue a declaratory sentence against them.[19] They are subject to the penal law of the Church even though they are not subject to the penal law of the state or nation over which they rule. Hence a ruler of a nation who orders the persecution of priests incurs the penalties of canon 2343, provided that all the conditions requisite for incurring the censure are fulfilled.

By express enactment of the Code all minors who have not yet reached the age of puberty are not liable to *latae sententiae* penalties.[20] The law presumes that a boy reaches the status of puberty at the age of fourteen, and a girl at the age of twelve.[21]

[17] Canon 233.

[18] Ciprotti, "De iniuria et diffamatione in iure poenali ecclesiastico"—*Apollinaris*, X (1937), 70.

[19] Canon 2227, § 1.

[20] Canon 2230.

[21] Canon 88, § 2.

However, it is taught by many canonists that in criminal matters the age of puberty is to be taken as fourteen both for boys and for girls.[22] Therefore, if a child below the age of fourteen should strike a priest, even with malice in his heart, he would not thereby incur an excommunication, but the child should be punished by means of some reformative and educational means. But if the child was induced or commanded to commit this crime by someone who has passed the age of puberty, the penalty is incurred by the party guilty of the enticement or command. The exemption of *impuberes* from the incurring of *latae sententiae* penalties is not communicated to *puberes* when there is cooperation between these two classes of persons.

Article 3 — Orientals and the Penalty

It has been shown that clerics and religious of the Oriental Church enjoy the privilege of the canon.[23] But clerics and religious of the majority of the Oriental rites do not enjoy the privilege *sub censura*. This means that if an Oriental subject should strike or injure a priest of his own rite he would not incur the censure of excommunication unless in the canon law of that rite such a penalty was attached to the commission of that crime. In that case a subject of an Oriental rite would incur whatever penalties are enacted in the law for malicious injury done to a priest. What, then, must be said of a Latin subject who would maliciously mutilate or injure an Oriental cleric or religious? Since canon 2343 does not qualify the terms "cleric" and "religious" it seems that a Latin who lays violent hands on *any* cleric or religious, be he Latin or Oriental, would be excommunicated.

In this connection it is now to be determined to what extent Orientals are liable to the censures of canon 2343. The general rule is that Orientals do not fall within the scope of the law of the Code except in matters which of their very nature *(ex ipsa*

22 Cappello, *De Censuris*, p. 19. But cf. Ojetti, *Commentarium*, lib. II, excursus ad can. 88, nn. 1-3.

23 *Supra*, pp. 72-73.

rei natura) affect also the Oriental Church.[24] This same rule, of course, is applicable to the penal regulations of the Code.

By specific declaration of the Holy Office it was decreed that the *specialissimo modo* reserved excommunication for laying violent hands on the person of the Supreme Pontiff extended to the universal Church.[25] The Holy Office in its reply stated that, in view of the utterly extraordinary gravity of the crime, this sanction is extended to the universal Church, the Latin and the Oriental of whatsoever rite.[26]

Even before this response was given there could scarcely be any doubt that the preceptive norm inherently corresponding to this penal canon affected all the faithful alike. Orientals as well as Latins must respect the clerical state. But the penalty as such is separable from the positive precept which demands that the clerical state be respected. No penalty, however, and much less a specific penalty, is in any way demanded by way of inherent consequence, since all penalties are based on justice and are inflicted for the welfare of society. The practical import of this principle could be that Orientals were not subject to this *specialissimo modo* reserved excommunication without the issuance of this decree.[27]

In the reply it was indicated that the competent authority for taking cognizance of this crime was the Holy Office as regarded the external forum. According to this same decree the cognizance of this crime, to be taken in the internal forum is reserved to the Sacred Penitentiary. There is no other authority in the Roman Curia competent to handle matters pertaining to the internal forum; not even the Sacred Congregation for the Oriental Church handles those matters in connection with Orientals.

The question is definitely settled as far as the *specialissimo modo* reserved censure enacted against malicious strikers of the

24 Canon 1.

25 S. C. S. Off., 21 iul. 1934—*AAS,* XXVI (1934), 550.

26 "Emi et Revmi Domini Cardinales . . . decreverunt . . . sanctiones (2330; 2343, § 1; 2367; 2369) extendi ad universam Ecclesiam Latinam et Orientalem cuiuscumque ritus."

27 Roberti, "Adnotationes"—*Apollinaris,* VIII (1935), 30.

Pope is concerned. But the problem concerning the possibility of Orientals incurring the excommunication for laying violent hands on clerics of a rank below that of the Roman Pontiff is left unsolved. If there is a censure established in the canon law of some particular rite, then the censure is incurred according to the norms of that law. In this country a very practical problem presents itself. There are many Orientals in the United States who have been committed to the care of Latin ordinaries.[28] The question could arise whether one of these Orientals when guilty of striking a religious or a cleric of the Latin rite, or that Latin bishop to whom he is subject, would be excommunicated. Herman holds that Orientals living in Latin territory are subject to the enacted penalties of the Code of Canon Law if the transgression of the law causes injury or public scandal in the place where the offense is committed.[29] But this principle cannot be accepted; its practical application would be laden with too many difficulties. This would seem to make these Orientals subject to most of the penalties of the Code. This principle would certainly make Orientals living in Latin territory subject to the censures established for violations of the privilege of the canon, for such violations would usually cause damage or public scandal.

In practice it can be said that Orientals are not subject to the penalties of canon 2343, except of course the *specialissimo modo* reserved censure. The argument for this is based on the fact that Orientals are bound only to those laws of the Latin Code which make express mention of them or which affect them *ex ipsa rei natura.*[30] The lesser malice inherent in an assault upon anyone inferior to the Pope leaves it problematical that the very gravity and heinousness of the assault inherently subjects all the faithful, even the Orientals for whom the Latin Code is not primarily intended, to the censure which the Latin Code establishes. Hence, here as in other penalties wherein the very gravity of the crime

28 Leo XIII, litt. ap. "*Orientalium dignitas,*" 30 nov. 1894, n. IX — *Fontes,* n. 627.

29 Herman, "De ritu in iure canonico" — *Orientalia Christiana* (Romae, 1923-1934), XXXII (1933), 156. Cf. Cicognani, *Canon Law,* p. 458.

30 Cf. canon 1.

does not postulate subjection to the censure on the part of all alike, Orientals are not liable to the censure for the reason that no consideration brings them under the Code law: neither the fact of any express mention of them in the law, nor the fact that the very nature of the crime demands their subjection to the penal law.

Article 4 — Conditions Requisite for the Incurring of the Censure

A. *Subjective Conditions*

Through the reception of first tonsure or through incorporation in the religious life a person is dedicated to the service of God. From then on because of his dedication to the divine ministry such a one is known as a *persona sacra.* His person, then, as something sacred is inviolable, and any desecration of it is sacrilegious.

A sacrilege is traditionally defined as the violation of a sacred object.[31] In this definition an object can be a person, place or thing which is dedicated to divine worship. Any irreverence which is shown towards a sacred person, place or thing constitutes a sacrilege. When a person is the object of the irreverence it is specifically a personal sacrilege.[32]

There are various ways in which a person can become guilty of a personal sacrilege, but this study is concerned only with the personal sacrilege which is committed by the laying of violent hands on ecclesiastical persons. This sacrilege has been constituted by law as a special delict.[33] Canon 119 states it thus: "the faithful become tainted with the delict of sacrilege, whenever they inflict a real injury on clerics." [34]

31 St. Thomas Aquinas, *Summa Theologica* (6 vols., Taurini: Marietti, 1932), 2a, 2æ, q. 99, a. 1.

32 Genicot-Salsmans, *Institutiones Theologiae Moralis* (13. ed., 2 vols., Bruxellis: L'Édition Universelle, 1936), I, 218; Prümmer, *Manuale Theologiae Moralis* (8. ed., recognita a E. M. Münch, 3 vols., Friburgi Brisgoviae: Herder, 1935-1936), II, 432.

33 Canons 2195 and 2343.

34 ". . . seque sacrilegii delicto commaculant, si quando clericis realem iniuriam intulerint." The translation is the writer's.

The penalties to be incurred for this delict of sacrilege are enacted in canon 2343. As regards the penalty of excommunication enacted in this canon the ordinary rules contained in the Code concerning the incurring of censures must be applied. There must first of all be a *delictum* in the sense of canon 2195, § 1, i. e., an external morally imputable violation of the law to which a penalty is attached. Imputability depends either on the element of bad intent *(dolus* as defined in canon 2200, § 1),[35] or on the element of culpability manifest through ignorance or neglect.[36] The causes which by their influence on the intellect or on the will diminish or exclude either of these elements in crime affect its imputability. The various effects of such causes are clearly expressed in the Code.[37] One must consider the mental or psychological element in order to determine whether or not a *latae sententiae* penalty is incurred. Canon 2229 gives the principles for the determination of the effect of ignorance, fear, drunkenness, passion, carelessness and mental weakness on the incurring of *latae sententiae* penalties.

These principles as taken from the penal law of the Code have an immediate bearing in connection with the excommunication incurred by those who maliciously strike clerics. To incur this censure a man must be responsible for his action. This excommunication can be incurred only by a delinquent who acts knowingly and willingly *(sciens et volens)*, with malice *(dolus)*, and with the intention of inflicting an injury *(animus iniuriandi)*.[38] The subjective gravity, therefore, depends on the knowledge, the freedom and the deliberation which characterize the act. The action by which the injury is inflicted must arise from a malicious intention and a deliberate will, so that the evil-doer cannot be excused from mortal sin.[39]

35 "Dolus heic est deliberata voluntas violandi legem, eique opponitur ex parte intellectus defectus cognitionis et ex parte voluntatis defectus libertatis."

36 Canon 2199.

37 Canons 2201 to 2207.

38 Kuttner, *Schuldlehre*, p. 73.

39 Pirhing, *Jus Canonicum Nova Methodo Explicatum* (5 vols. in 3, Dilingae, 1722), Lib. V, tit. xxxix, n. 50; Hollweck, *Die kirchlichen Straf-*

Only those who are formally guilty of a grave sin of sacrilege, committed through the laying of violent hands on clerics or on religious, are subject to the incurring of the *latae sententiae* excommunications enacted in canon 2343. If there is present some condition which excuses from mortal sin, the penalty is not incurred. Furthermore the sin must be formally sacrilegious, i. e., the doer of the act must be aware that the person on whom he is inflicting the injury is a cleric or a religious.[40]

From the principles just enumerated it is clear that the law contemplates instances when to lay hands on a cleric or a religious would not be considered violent. In such cases the striking of one who enjoys the privilege may be justified either for the reason that there is no malice *(dolus)* or culpability *(culpa)*, or inasmuch as the act of striking the person is warranted on some licit title. The law of the Code does not cite examples, but in the law prevailing prior to the enactment of the Code the occasions when the striking of a cleric or of a religious was considered justified or free from sin were carefully specified, chiefly through Decretal legislation. These Decretal laws in which examples are given still retain their force, for they are in accord with the general principles of the new Code.

An ecclesiastical superior was permitted to chastise his clerical or religious subjects even if they were in major Orders.[41] There had to be a proportionate cause for this punishment and the chastisement itself had to be moderate and not done with an instrument that was likely to inflict serious bodily harm. In modern times this method of punishing errant clerics or religious is outmoded.

gesetze, § 148, n. 3; Grandclaude, *Jus Canonicum* (3 vols., Parisiis, 1882-1883), III, 602; Cappello, *De Censuris,* p. 327; Eichmann, *Das Strafrecht des Codex Iuris Canonici* (Paderborn: Schöningh, 1920), p. 166.

40 Cerato, *Censurae Vigentes Ipso Facto a Codice Iuris Canonici Excerptae* (2. ed., Patavii: Typis Seminarii, 1921), p. 97 (hereafter cited *Censurae Vigentes).*

41 C. 10, 54, X, *de sententia excommunicationis,* V, 39. Cf. Gonzalez-Tellez, *Commentaria Perpetua in Singulos Textus Quinque Librorum Decretalium Gregorii IX* (5 vols., Venetiis, 1756), lib. V, tit. 39, c. 1, n. 4; Ojetti, *Commentarium,* lib. II, ad can. 119, n. 5.

In a similar manner parents could for disciplinary reasons strike or whip their son who was a cleric or a religious. This right of parents, however, did not seem to extend to clerics who had already received major Orders.[42] What has been said about parents applied also to school teachers who had clerics or religious as pupils.[43]

To strike a cleric or a religious in a jocose manner involved no sin. The absence of sin, of course, precluded the incurring of the censure.[44] The purpose of the privilege of the canon, now as then, is to protect clerics and religious against malicious injury, not against that which results in a spirit of levity or fun. Consequently, if two clerics in a spirit of fun should begin to exchange blows, then through the blows which are exchanged there does not result any malicious injury. This is true even if one of the participants should suffer some slight injury, such as a cut or a nosebleed.

Likewise anyone who strikes a cleric in self-defense is clear of all blame, and therefore does not incur the censure. The law of nature permits anyone to use force against an unjust aggressor, even though the aggressor belongs to the hierarchy.[45] In defending himself, however, a man may not exceed the bounds of justifiable protection *(moderamen inculpatae tutelae)*. He may use only such means as he deems necessary to ward off the aggressor. The law of self-defense would permit a person to snatch, even violently, from a cleric or a religious an instrument which he might need for his own defense. So, v. g., if a man was being pursued by another man carrying a gun, he might eject a priest from his automobile in order to use it to escape his ag-

42 C. 54, X *de sententia excommunicationis,* V, 39. Cf. Reiffenstuel, lib. V, tit. 39, n. 123; Maupied, *Juris Canonici Compendium,* II, 64, n. VIII. Cappello *(De Censuris,* p. 328), following Suarez *(De Censuris in Communi,* disp. xxii, sect. i, n. 49), holds that this right of the parents extends to a child of theirs even when constituted in major Orders.

43 C. 1, X, *de sententia excommunicationis,* V, 39.

44 C. 1, X, *de sententia excommunicationis,* V, 39.

45 Pope Alexander III (1159-1181) in enacting this law stated: "quum vim cum vi repellere, omnes leges omniaque iura permittant." — C. 3, X, *de sententia excommunicationis,* V, 39. Cf. canon 2205, § 4.

gressor.[46] This would be a case of extreme necessity, and hence the law which forbids all real injury to clerics would be suspended. In self-defense many things become licit which under ordinary circumstances would be illicit. So it is permitted to strike a cleric or a religious in defense of an innocent third party, but these defense measures can be taken only at the precise moment that the cleric or the religious is actually physically assaulting the innocent party. It is also considered a just means of self-defense for a man forcibly to eject a cleric or a religious from his home, if the priest or the religious on his visit at the home was causing disturbances or quarrels.[47]

There is no violation of the privilege of the canon in the following case. A cleric or a religious cannot claim the right to protection in virtue of his privilege if in defiling his clerical chastity he be apprehended in the act of sin with the wife, mother, sister or daughter of someone.[48] The person who strikes the cleric may indeed be guilty of grave sin for attacking the cleric even under these circumstances, but he does not incur the excommunication for the reason that the legislator, taking into consideration the detestable nature of the sin and also the great difficulty the cleric's assaulter would encounter in restraining the sudden and almost uncontrollable impulse of anger and revenge, excuses the assaulter from incurring the censure.[49]

For the same reason Cappello states that the assaulter does not fall under excommunication if he should strike the cleric or the religious, even though the latter is not apprehended directly in the act of sin, but under strongly suspicious circumstances is found to be alone with the woman. Cappello likewise thinks it probable that anyone is excused from excommunication if he strikes a cleric or a religious who is discovered committing a sin of immorality with any woman.[50]

[46] For the principle involved in this example cf. Suarez, *De Censuris in Communi*, disp. xxii, sect. I, n. 38.

[47] Reiffenstuel, lib. V, tit. 39, n. 120.

[48] C. 3, X, *de sententia excommunicationis*, V, 39.

[49] Schmalzgrueber, lib. V, tit. 39, n. 237.

[50] *De Censuris*, p. 328.

Also if a women strikes a cleric or a religious who solicits her, she is not excommunicated, provided that she cannot repel him or has no means of escape.[51] St. Alphonsus admits that a woman may strike a cleric if he be so importune in his solicitation of her that she cannot repulse him by means of crying out against him, but solely on the assumption that through such a solicitation she is brought to the verge of a lapse against the virtue of purity at least by way of an ultimate wilful harboring of impure thought.[52]

The censure with which those who are guilty of physical assault and attack on clerics or on religious are punished is attached to a formal sin of sacrilege. A material sin of sacrilege is not punished with excommunication.[53] This is an important distinction, for it implies that in order to be guilty of formal sacrilege, the malicious striker of clerics must recognize that the person whom he is about to assault is a cleric or a religious. If the man intend to strike a lay person and by mistake hit a cleric or a religious he would not be excommunicated.[54]

There has been a long-standing controversy whether a person would be excommunicated if he had in mind to injure some particular cleric, but actually inflicted the injury on a cleric or a religious whom he did not intend to harm. The question is whether Mr. Jackson would be excommunicated if, intending to fight Father Smith, he actually engaged in a fist-fight with Father Brown because of mistaken identity.[55] In practice it seems best to hold that Mr. Jackson is not excommunicated, for since he actually intended to strike Father Smith, his striking of Father Brown was only accidental. Mr. Jackson, of course, is obliged to use sufficient diligence to prevent such a mistake from occurring. It seems to be the better opinion that he would

51 C. 3, X, *de sententia excommunicationis*, V, 39.

52 *Theologia Moralis*, lib. VII, n. 275, 6.

53 Coronata, *Institutiones*, IV, 426.

54 C. 4, X, *de sententia excommunicationis*, V, 39.

55 Kuttner, *Schuldlehre*, pp. 180-184; Suarez, *De Censuris in Communi*, disp. xxii, dect. I, n. 54; Cavigioli, *De Censuris*, p. 130; Cipollini, *De Censuris*, p. 120; Cappello, *De Censuris*, p. 327; Augustine, *A Commentary on Canon Law*, VIII, 378.

not be excommunicated in view of the principle that all penal law is to be interpreted strictly.[56] In addition to this it can be said that there is question of a dubious penalty, in which case the more favorable interpretation should be adopted.[57]

B. Objective Conditions

The censure of excommunication enacted against malicious assaulters of clerics or of religious is not incurred unless in the assault there is shown some disrespect to the clerical or the religious state. Although for the incurring of the censure this disparagement to the dignity of the clerical or the religious state must actually be present, it is not necessary that the culprit consciously intend this. In order that the culprit incur the censure it is sufficient that he be aware that the victim of his attack is a cleric or a religious. A malicious assault upon a cleric or a religious is always considered injurious to the prestige and dignity of the clerical or the religious state, even though the culprit does not specifically advert to it.[58]

In the preceding section of the present article it was shown that the censure incurred through the malicious striking of clerics or of religious presupposes a grave sin of sacrilege. In the present section the objective nature of the crime punishable with the censure enacted in canon 2343 will be discussed.

According to the express legislation of the Code only a grave, external, consummated (or complete) delinquency combined with contumacy is punished with censures.[59] Of all the ecclesiastical penalties censures are the most severe, and for that reason they can be incurred only for external acts which are grievously culpable. Moreover, excommunication which is the most drastic of the censures is enacted only for those who are guilty of the most serious disorders. To incur an excommunication, therefore, a person must have committed both objectively and subjectively a mortal sin.

56 Canon 19.
57 Canon 2219, § 1.
58 Cavigioli, *De Censuris*, p. 55.
59 Canon 2242, § 1.

Considering crime objectively, the legislator indicates that the first requisite for the incurring of a censure is that the crime itself must be of a grave nature. By applying this principle to the excommunication enacted against the *percussores clericorum* one can state that the excommunication is not incurred unless the assault against the cleric or the religious is gravely injurious. But in order that there be a grave injury as a result of this crime it is not necessary that there be a great intensity of pain or a serious physical injury.[60] The act of assault may be slight in itself, and yet be grave as an irreverence. Thus, to slap a priest would cause no serious wound and very little pain, and yet it would constitute a grave injury, if it were done out of malice. St. Alphonsus remarked that the striking of clerics is always considered gravely injurious because of the reverence that is due to the cleric, and for that reason even a slight assault consisting of the least physical contact is punishable with excommunication.[61]

Furthermore, it is not required that the injury be absolutely grave in itself regardless of all circumstances; it suffices that it be relatively grave. An objectively slight injury could for instance become a grave one in consequence of the special dignity of the person, the publicity of the crime, or the place in which the crime is committed. The question here is not one of greater or lesser mortal sin, but simply one of an act which under the circumstances makes the misdeed to be a mortal sin at all.[62]

To ascertain whether or not an act of violence is injurious, and consequently censurable, one must carefully consider whether the action according to the common estimate of men is considered to have gravely injured the dignity of the cleric or of the religious according as the case stands. An injury which is inflicted on a layman may under certain circumstances be considered trivial, whereas the same injury when inflicted under the

60 St. Alphonsus Liguori, *Theologia Moralis*, lib. VII, n. 275; Suarez, *De Censuris in Communi*, disp. xxii, sect. 1, n. 25.

61 *Loc. cit.*

62 Coronata, *Institutiones*, IV, 427; Hollweck, *Die kirchlichen Strafgesetze*, § 148, n. 6.

same circumstances on a priest would have to be considered grave.[63] Thus violently to snatch an object from a cleric's hands or to pull his hair would constitute actions punishable with the censure of excommunication, whereas these same actions when perpetrated against a lay person might not be mortally sinful.[64]

The second element which must be verified in a crime is that it must be external, for internal sinful acts are not punishable with censure.[65] It must be noted however that the criminal action can be external and at the same time occult.[66] If a priest were assaulted with no one present but himself and his assailant, the crime would indeed be occult but nevertheless external, and hence the culprit would be excommunicated provided that the assault was malicious.

Finally, the malicious action must be complete or consummated. The act requires that an act be complete in all its effects before a censure is incurred. Hence there is no threat of censure in the case of frustrated, attempted or incomplete crime.[67] On the basis of this principle it is obvious that if a cleric avoids the blow of an assailant the latter does not fall under excommunication.

In addition to the elements which must be verified in the criminal action, it is further required that the culprit be contumacious if he is to incur the censure.[68] In the case of *latae sententiae* penalties a person is considered to be contumacious when he knowingly and deliberately transgresses the law or the precept to which the *latae sententiae* penalty is attached. For the incurring, then, of the *latae sententiae* excommunication which is enacted against malicious strikers of clerics no previous canonical warning is necessary, since the penal law itself, threat-

63 Salucci, *Il Diritto Penale,* II, 170.

64 Reiffenstuel, lib. V, tit. 39, n. 117.

65 Heylen, *De Censuris* (4. ed., Mechliniae: H. Dessain, 1945), p. 24.

66 Augustine, *A Commentary on Canon Law,* VIII, 115.

67 Ciprotti, "De consummatione delictorum attento eorum elemento obiectivo" — *Apollinaris,* VIII (1935), 229-230.

68 Canon 2242, § 1.

ening the penalty to be incurred *ipso facto,* contains this admonition.[69]

The action punishable with the excommunication mentioned in canon 2343 is described as *"violentas manus iniicere."* This is a metaphorical expression which signifies corporal injury in general.[70] On the other hand, canon 119, which emphasizes the positive aspect of the privilege of the canon, indicates that a *realis iniuria* inflicted on clerics constitutes a delict of sacrilege. The use of these two different expressions by the legislator in reference to the same clerical privilege does not imply that a different kind of action is required to incur the excommunication than to be guilty of the delict of sacrilege. Because of the relationship between the two canons the inflicting of a real (physical) injury on a cleric and the laying of violent hands on a cleric must be interpreted as implying the same kind of physical injury.[71]

The violence or injurious bodily assault on clerics which is punishable with an excommunication to be incurred *ipso facto* must be committed by some physical deed against the person of the cleric or the religious; otherwise no excommunication is incurred. There must be an external, sinful action committed against the physical nature or constitution of a person who enjoys the privilege of the canon, or the things or objects in direct contact with his person.[72] Contumely, verbal insults or threats, and libel are not punishable with the excommunication of which mention is made in canon 2343.

For an attack on a cleric or a religious to be censurable there must be immediate or mediate physical contact with the person of the cleric or the religious. The physical contact is immediate when the injury directly affects the body of the cleric or the

69 Cerato, *Censurae Vigentes,* p. 7.

70 Fallon, "The Privilege of the Canon,"—*Irish Ecclesiastical Record,* 5. series, LI (1938), p. 75.

71 Ojetti, *Commentarium,* lib. II, ad. can. 119, n. 4; Kuttner, *Schuldlehre,* p. 73.

72 Coronata, *Institutiones,* IV, 425; Maroto, *Institutiones Iuris Canonici ad Normam Novi Codicis* (2 vols., Vol. I, Romae: Matriti, 1919), I, 594.

religious.[73] Violence of this kind would be exemplified in the act of striking a cleric with or without an instrument, of kicking him, of mutilating him, of drenching him, of pelting him with stones or other objects, etc. Since the law indicates that the act of laying violent hands on the person of a cleric or a religious must be violent, it can be concluded that the theft of some object from a cleric or a religious does not constitute a violation of the privilege of the canon, for in theft there is no act of violence. Robbery, on the other hand, would constitute a violation of the privilege of the canon, for in robbery violence is implied. Thus, violently and forcefully to snatch something from the hand of a priest is an action forbidden by canon 119.

The physical contact is said to be mediate when the act of physical violence only indirectly inflicts harm on the person of the cleric or the religious. The words *"violentas manus iniicere"* do not imply that it is necessary that the cleric's body be immediately or directly touched. To administer a dose of poison to a priest is a violation of the privilege of the canon, although there is no physical contact between the poisoner and his victim. But with reference to the act of poisoning a cleric or a religious it is commonly taught that the excommunication is not incurred until the poison actually begins to take effect.[74]

As a general rule it can be stated that any assault which has the effect of gravely injuring the honor or dignity of the cleric according to common estimation is to be considered a grave injury. Thus if the clothes or the clerical insignia which the cleric is wearing, or the horse on which or the automobile in which he is riding, is the immediate object of attack there can be a violation of the privilege of the canon. Deliberately to cause a cleric to fall, or to incite a dog to bite him are also actions which reap for the delinquent the penalties of canon 2343.[75]

The person of a cleric or of a religious is considered to be

73 Cavigioli, *De Censuris*, p. 56.

74 St. Alphonsus Liguori, *Theologia Moralis*, lib. VIII, n. 280; Heylen, *De Censuris*, p. 157.

75 Cavigioli, *De Censuris*, p. 56; Sole, *De Delictis et Poenis*, n. 377.

the object of a physical attack, at least indirectly, when his liberty is restrained or interfered with in any way. Wherefore, arrest and imprisonment of one who enjoys the privilege of the canon are, strictly considered, restraints upon his liberty, and consequently imply violations of the privilege. The Church claims sole authority over those who enjoy the clerical privileges, and any intrusion upon their liberty is considered as an intrusion upon the Church's authority. But this does not mean that an officer of the civil law is forbidden to arrest a cleric or a religious whom he apprehends in the act of perpetrating a crime, of committing a misdemeanor, or of disturbing the peace. According to canonical teaching the officer is to arrest such a cleric and turn him over to ecclesiastical authority for punishment.[76]

Wilful detention of one who enjoys the privilege of the canon is also forbidden to private authority. Thus, if a cleric is forcibly detained in some dwelling, be it public or private, his captors and detainers are subject to the ecclesiastical penalties, provided that their actions are malicious. In this connection it may be observed that for the incurring of the penalties enacted in canon 2343 it is not postulated that physical force be used when the cleric or the religious is taken prisoner, but it suffices that when the cleric or the religious has freely come to a place he then be detained there by force. If, for instance, parishioners in protest against the removal of their pastor should decide to prevent his removal by holding him in the rectory as a prisoner, the parties guilty of the act would be excommunicated, even though a finger had never been lifted against the pastor.

With regard to the arrest and the imprisonment by civil authority of those who enjoy the privilege of the canon Sebastianelli (†1920) remarked that the Church's teaching concerning the common privilege of clerics has at least partially been derogated by contrary custom, by concordat law, and *de facto* by the malice or positive indifference of civil governments.[77] Indeed, as late as the year 1930 Sägmüller (1860-1942) observed that in

76 C. 3, 35, X, *de sententia excommunicationis,* V, 39. Cf. Schmalzgrueber, lib. V, tit. 39, n. 231.

77 *Praelectiones Juris Canonici,* I *(De Personis),* p. 16.

modern civil law the privilege of the canon as such has almost completely disappeared.[78] That the privilege of the canon in modern times has lost much of its significance, and in many cases is entirely disregarded in public social life, is a fact substantiated by the atrocities committed against clerics and religious in recent times.[79]

In the United States, however, clergymen hold a very honored position and are accorded greater respect than is given to men of other professions. Evidences of the respect shown to clerics and religious are seen in the courtesies shown them, such as, for example, the exemption from conscription into the armed forces. Although the civil authority has not for the most part been wanting in manifesting respect to the clergy, nonetheless the fact that a person is a cleric does not entitle him to rights not possessed by other citizens, nor is he immune to the ordinary application of law.[80]

Neither the Federal Government nor the government of any of the States takes cognizance of the Church's teaching regarding the privilege of the canon. Consequently, if a priest or any other person who enjoys the privilege of the canon is guilty of an infraction of the civil law he is liable to arrest and to the same penalties as any other citizen as far as the civil law is concerned. This legal principle is, indeed, alien to the canonical doctrine concerning the privilege of the canon; but one who observes the practical application of law in this country must admit that the rigor of this law is mitigated to some extent in actual practice. However, officers of the law as well as other civil authorities who arrest and imprison clerics or religious in accordance with the provisions of the civil law in most cases probably would not incur the penalties enacted for violations of the privilege of the canon because of ignorance.

78 *Lehrbuch des katholischen Kirchenrechts*, Vol. I, Pars III, p. 338.

79 Cf. *The Catholic Review* (Washington, D. C., 1936—), X (1945), No. 31, p. 10; No. 32, p. 1. Pope Pius XII has recently expressed his sorrow for the sufferings of priests and religious in Poland.—*AAS*, XXXVII (1945), 205-206.

80 Zollman, *American Church Law* (St. Paul: West Publishing Company, 1933), p. 428.

CHAPTER IX

THE VARIOUS DEGREES OF THE CRIME OF THE VIOLATION OF THE PRIVILEGE OF THE CANON

ARTICLE 1 — MALICIOUS ASSAULT UPON THE POPE AND ITS PUNISHMENT

Canon 2343, §1. Qui violentas manus in personam Romani Pontificis iniecerit:

1°. *Excommunicationem contrahit latae sententiate Sedi Apostolicae specialissimo modo reservatam; et est ipso facto vitandus;*

2°. *Est ipso iure infamis;*

3°. *Clericus est degradandus.*

A. The Censure of Excommunication

Among other circumstances which may increase the imputability of a delinquency and the gravity of a crime is the dignity or the character of the person against whom the delinquency or crime is committed.[1] This principle of law is axiomatically expressed in the well-known words: *"iniuria est in persona iniuriata."*[2] In its application in ecclesiastical law this principle indicates that the higher the person stands in the hierarchy, or the greater the respect that is due to him, the greater also is the offense committed against him. The moral gravity of a physical injury suffered by a person who enjoys the privilege of the canon will vary in proportion to the greater or lesser dignity of the injured party. Observing this principle the legislator punishes violators of the privilege of the canon according to the degree of dignity the injured person has attained in the hierarchy of orders or of jurisdiction.

1 Canon 2207, 1°

2 The axiom is cited thus in Salucci, *Il Diritto Penale,* II, 170. Cf. St. Thomas Aquinas, *In X Libros Ethicorum ad Nicomachum,* Lib. I, lect. V — *Omnia Opera* (34 Vols., Parisiis, 1871-1887), Vol. XXV, 245. The Glossators have expressed this principle in the following manner: "ex persona augetur crimen." — *Glossa Ordinaria* ad c. 14, X, *de sententia excommunicationis,* V, 39, s. v. "asperior."

The highest person in dignity and power in the Church is Christ's vicar, the Pope. There can be little doubt that an attack upon the person of the Supreme Pontiff would constitute the crime of *lèse majesté,* although there is no specific statement to this effect in the law. But if those who imprison Cardinals or treat them with violence are guilty of this crime,[3] it can be concluded *a fortiori* that those guilty of a similar offense against the Pope can also be accused of the crime of *lèse majesté.*[4]

Before all discussion of the ecclesiastical penalties to be invoked against those who maliciously infringe on the Pope's personal inviolability, mention may be made of pertinent matter contained in the *"Leggi della Città del Vaticano."* These laws were promulgated on June 7, 1929, following the ratification of the Concordat between the Holy See and the Italian Government. In this body of laws the death penalty is decreed against anyone who in the territory of Vatican City commits any deed against the life, the integrity, or the personal liberty of the Supreme Pontiff.[5] In the Concordat between the Holy See and Italy, the Italian Government agreed to consider the person of the Supreme Pontiff as sacred and inviolable, and any public offenses and injuries committed against him in Italian territory were to be treated as offenses and injuries against the person of the King.[6]

For the first time in the history of canon law the Code establishes a specific censure to be incurred by those who trespass against the personal inviolability of the Pope.[7] Because of the seriousness of this crime the Church has evoked her most drastic penalties against such offenders. A crime of this nature would indicate utter contempt for the highest ecclesiastical authority, and would bespeak at the same time an attempt to undermine that authority. The Church therefore uses every means at her disposal to forestall such an attempt.

3 C. 5, *de poenis,* V, 9, in VI°. Cf. *supra,* p. 35.

4 Vermeersch-Creusen, *Epitome,* III, n. 542.

5 Salucci, *Il Diritto Penale,* II, 171, n. 1.

6 *AAS,* XXI (1929), 213.

7 Cappello, *De Censuris,* p. 195.

A person who is guilty of a felonious assault against the Pope is punished first of all with an excommunication for which absolution is reserved in a very special way *(specialissimo modo)* to the Holy See. An excommunication which is reserved in this manner to the Holy See for absolution does not differ in its canonical effects from an excommunication which is reserved to the Holy See in a special way or in a simple way. The difference between these three types of reservation is to be found in the different kinds of faculties which are required for the absolution of the censures.[8] Very special faculties from the Sacred Penitentiary are necessary for the granting of absolution from a censure which is reserved in a very special way. In granting such faculties the Sacred Penitentiary is exacting in its demands from the penitent, and severe in its imposition of penances.[9] This, of course, is due to the very serious nature of the crime for which the censure is imposed.

Even in the most ample general faculties the power to absolve from a censure which is reserved *specialissimo modo* is not granted. An exception to this rule is made only in the faculties which grant any priest the power to absolve persons who are in danger of death,[10] and in the faculties granted to any confessor whereby he can give absolution in the more urgent and pressing cases according to the norms of canon 2254. The power to absolve from a censure reserved in a very special way to the Holy See is excluded, for example, from the faculties granted to Cardinals,[11] bishops[12] and ordinaries.[13]

The Code in several instances indicates the severity of the Church in dealing with crimes which are punishable with an excommunication reserved to the Holy See in a very special way. Such an excommunication, for example, cannot be absolved validly by a confessor who is in ignorance of the reservation.[14]

8 Regatillo, *Institutiones Iuris Canonici,* II, 363.

9 Coronata, *Institutiones,* IV, 162.

10 Canon 2252.

11 Canon 239, § 1, 1°.

12 Canon 349, § 1.

13 Canon 2237, § 2.

14 Canon 2247, § 3.

A priest who without the necessary faculties presumes to absolve from an excommunication reserved to the Holy See in a very special way would himself incur an excommunication reserved to the Holy See in a special manner.[15] Finally, the strictness of the Church in this matter is seen in the obligation of recourse which is imposed under pain of the reincurring of the censure when absolution from such a censure is given in danger of death and the party so absolved survives,[16] or when the absolution is given in virtue of the faculties granted in canon 2254, for the more urgent and pressing cases.

When a person incurs an excommunication because of an assault upon the person of the Pope, he is also branded as a *vitandus*.[17] As an exception to canon 2258, § 2, the canon which establishes the penalties incurred by those who lay violent hands on the Pope states that a person guilty of this crime becomes *ipso facto vitandus*. Ordinarily a person does not become an *excommunicatus vitandus* unless three conditions are fulfilled: 1) he must be excommunicated by name by the Apostolic See; 2) the excommunication must be publicly proclaimed; and 3) in the decree or sentence it must be expressly stated that the person is to be avoided. The law however waives all these formalities in the case of a person guilty of a felonious assault upon the Supreme Pontiff. Hence the very act of striking the Pope maliciously, even though it be occult, of itself causes the delinquent to become a *vitandus*. But as long as knowledge regarding the malicious act remains occult the faithful are not bound by the obligation of avoiding the excommunicate. This obligation begins only when they first learn of the criminal act.[18]

B. The Vindicative Penalties

In the discussion concerning the censure of excommunication incurred *ipso facto* through a malicious assault upon the Pope,

15 Canon 2238, § 1.

16 Canon 2252.

17 Canon 2343, § 1, 1°.

18 Cappello, *De Censuris*, p. 140; Coronata, *Institutiones*, IV, 193.

it was indicated that this censure is the first of its kind in the long history of canon law. The statement that never before was there a specific censure enacted against those who inflicted a real injury on the Pope is supported with sufficient authority. But the opinion is here advanced that neither were there any vindicative penalties enacted for this crime in the law which prevailed prior to the publication of the Code of Canon Law. As far as the writer has been able to ascertain, no vindicative penalties enacted for this crime are to be found in the law of the Decretals. Moreover, canonical writers on the Decretal law make no reference to such penalties when they discuss the privilege of the canon. The writer's opinion, advanced with some hesitancy in view simply of the absence of any positive statement in the writings of canonists on the past as well as the present law, seems justified also when one considers that the gravity of this crime would have demanded the severest penalty at the disposal of the Church. If this crime had been considered specifically as an object of any kind of punishment in the old law, it is reasonable to assume that an excommunication would have been specifically established by the law. If the crime had been considered specifically as an object of punishment in the old law, it does not seem likely that the Church would overlook excommunication and establish less severe penalties.

Although there was no excommunication specifically enacted against those who presumed to attack the Pope, nevertheless a person who was guilty of this crime before the Code, incurred the excommunication enacted against those persons who violated the personal immunity of a bishop, since the Pope was then, as now, the Bishop of Rome. The Church could also have exercised her coercive power on specific occasions and thus have inflicted other penalties on those who dared to attack the Pope.

The Code of Canon Law, however, has established besides the censures already noted certain vindicative penalties which are incurred by those who violate the person of the Pope. In addition to the censure of excommunication, which is incurred through the malicious striking of the Pope, there is attached to this same crime the vindicative penalty of legal infamy. Like the censure of excommunication, the penalty of legal infamy is incurred *ipso facto*.[19] The juridic effects of this penalty are definitely established in canon 2294, § 1. They are as follows:

1. Infamy of law produces an irregularity in consequence of which no layman can receive the tonsure and no cleric can receive any higher Orders, or apart from an apostolic dispensation exercise even those he already has received.[20]

2. Legal infamy entails disqualification for any ecclesiastical benefice, pension, office, or dignity. If any of these is conferred before a dispensation from the penalty has been obtained, the conferral is invalid.[21]

3. A person who has incurred the penalty of legal infamy is incapacitated for the performance of any of the legally authorized ecclesiastical acts, mention of which is made in canon 2256, 2°.[22]

4. Legal infamy prevents a person from exercising any ecclesiastical right or charge. This prohibition prevents a person from exercising such rights as that of election, presentation, nomination, etc. The person also is prohibited from exercising such charges as are involved in the offices of notaries, defenders, procurators or attorneys, administrators, etc.[23]

5. A person who is legally infamous is not permitted to take an active part in the ministry of the sacred functions. Thus,

19 Canon 2343, § 1, 2°.

20 Cf. Cappello, *Tractatus Canonico-Moralis de Sacramentis* (3 vols. in 6, Taurinorum Augustae: Marietti, 1932-1939; Vol. II, 1935), II, Pars II, 416. Cf. canons 983; 984, 5°.

21 Cf. Woywod, *A Practical Commentary on the Code of Canon Law* (8. ed., revised by Callistus Smith, 2 vols., New York: Jos. F. Wagner, Inc., 1944), II, 458.

22 Canon 2256, 2°: "Nomine autem actuum legitimorum ecclesiasticorum significantur: munus administratoris gerere bonorum ecclesiasticorum; partes agere iudicis, auditoris et relatoris, defensoris vinculi, promotoris iustitiae et fidei, notarii et cancellarii, cursoris et apparitoris, advocati et procuratoris in causis ecclesiasticis; munus patrini agere in sacramentis baptismi et confirmationis; suffragium ferre in electionibus ecclesiasticis; ius patronatus exercere."

23 Augustine, *A Commentary on Canon Law*, VIII, 246-247.

serving at Holy Mass, carrying the cross, playing the organ at divine services, etc., are acts which are forbidden to him.

If a person who lays violent hands on the Pope incurs the penalty of legal infamy and is later judicially declared to be legally infamous, he is restricted from acting validly as a sponsor in baptism[24] or in confirmation.[25] After the declaratory sentence a person who is legally infamous also loses his right to vote in canonical elections,[26] as well as his right to exercise his ecclesiastical patronage.[27] A person marked with infamy through the pronouncement of a declaratory sentence cannot validly act in the capacity of a private judge *(arbiter)* on an issue submitted to him by mutual agreement of the contending parties,[28] nor may he be admitted in the capacity of a witness or of a specialist or expert in ecclesiastical trials, since he is considered suspect.[29]

The severity of this penalty can be seen in its juridic effects, as well as in its reservation to the Holy See for dispensation. Ordinarily the crime of laying violent hands on the person of the Supreme Pontiff would be public, and in that case the Holy See alone is competent to grant the dispensation from the penalty of legal infamy. But if in some rare instance the crime remained occult, then any ordinary could dispense from the legal infamy incurred because of the crime in virtue of the power granted to ordinaries in canon 2237, § 2.[30]

If the person who commits the crime in question is a cleric the Code specifically states that he is to be degraded. Although this penalty is of a *ferendae sententiae* character, the use of the form *degradandus est* indicates that it is a penalty which *must*

24 Canon 765, 2°.

25 Canon 795, 2°.

26 Canon 167, 3°.

27 Canon 1470, § 4.

28 Canon 1931.

29 Canons 1757, § 2; 1795.

30 Canon 2237, § 2: "In casibus vero occultis, firmo praescripto can. 2254 et 2290, potest Ordinarius poenas latae sententiae iure communi statutas per se vel per alium remittere, exceptis censuris specialissimo vel speciali modo Sedi Apostolicae reservatis."

be inflicted. In this case no option is given to the judge, so that he is not free to waive the application of this penalty.

Degradation, which is the severest vindicative penalty that the Church can inflict on errant clerics, includes deposition, the perpetual privation of the right to wear the clerical dress, and reduction to the lay state.[31] Deposition, while leaving intact both the obligations arising from the Orders already received and also the clerical privileges deriving from these Orders, implies a suspension from office and a disqualification for any offices, dignities, benefices, pensions, or charges in the Church. Any office, dignity, benefice, pension, or charge which a guilty cleric already has, is forfeited even though he was ordained under its title.[32] Although no specific mention of the following factor is made in the law, nonetheless it is accepted as a common opinion that deposition strips a cleric of the lawful exercise of all the powers of Orders which he has received and, so to speak, places him on a par with the simple tonsured cleric who enjoys no power of Orders.[33] But as the Code itself indicates, the intrinsic power of Orders, if once validly received, is never taken away by deposition.[34] Moreover, since deposition takes away the very title by which a cleric has jurisdiction, any act of jurisdiction attempted thereafter by the deposed cleric is *ipso facto* invalid.[35]

The perpetual privation of the right to wear the ecclesiastical garb prohibits the exercise of any ecclesiastical functions by the person so punished, and also causes forfeiture of the clerical privileges.[36] The law which prohibits the exercise of any ecclesiastical ministry does not declare that any acts performed in contravention of this prohibition are invalid. Accordingly Augustine (1872-1943) stated that these acts are still valid, though illicit.[37]

31 Canon 2305, § 1.

32 Canon 2303, § 1.

33 Findlay, *Canonical Norms Governing the Deposition and Degradation of Clerics*, p. 144.

34 Canon 211, § 1.

35 Findlay, *op. cit.*, p. 150.

36 Canon 2300.

37 *A Commentary on Canon Law*, VIII, 259.

The distinctive feature of the penalty of degradation is that it reduces a cleric to the lay state. It matters not how far the cleric has advanced in the hierarchy of Orders or of jurisdiction, degradation will put him on a par with a lay person. This reduction to the lay state is, of course, of a merely legal or extrinsic character, for the power of sacred Orders can never be taken from a cleric. As canon 2305 states, degradation may be merely verbal (or by edict), when it is inflicted by sentence, or real, if the solemnities prescribed in the Roman Pontifical are observed. Both types of degradation have the same juridic effects.

Article 2 — Malicious Assault upon Cardinals, Legates, Patriarchs, Archbishops and Bishops and Its Punishment

Canon 2343, § 2. Qui in personam S. R. E. Cardinalis vel Legati Romani Pontificis [*violentas manus iniecerit*]:

1°. In excommunicationem incurrit latae sententiae Sedi Apostolicae speciali modo reservatam;

2° Est ipso iure infamis;

3° Privetur beneficiis, officiis, dignitatibus, pensionibus et quolibet munere, si quod in Ecclesia habeat.

§ 3. Qui in personam Patriarchae, Archiepiscopi etiam titularis tantum, incurrit in excommunicationem latae sententiae Sedi Apostolicae speciali modo reservatam.

A. The Censure of Excommunication

The present law attaches penal sanctions to the violation of the privilege of the canon in accordance with the general principle that a delict is increased in proportion to the greater dignity of the person offended.[38] When the offense is committed against the person of a Cardinal, a legate of the Roman Pontiff, a patriarch, an archbishop or a bishop (whether he be a residential bishop or only a titular bishop) the excommunication incurred is reserved *speciali modo* to the Holy See. Through this excommunication a person is excluded from communion with the faithful with all the legal consequences mentioned in the Code.[39]

[38] Canon 2207, 1°.

[39] Canon 2257, § 1. The legal effects of excommunication are mentioned in canons 2259 to 2267.

The legal consequences of the excommunication incurred through violences perpetrated against the person of a Cardinal, a papal legate, a patriarch, an archbishop or a bishop do not differ in any way from the legal effects of the excommunication incurred through similar violences perpetrated against the person of the Pope. The excommunication can be considered to be less severe to the extent that the power to absolve from the excommunication incurred through the violation of the privilege of the canon in the case of Cardinals, papal legates, etc., is more easily obtained, and the penances imposed are somewhat mollified.

The penalties enacted in canon 2343 for the laying of violent hands on the person of a Cardinal are not incurred unless the Pope has created the Cardinal and has published his name in a consistory.[40] A public announcement of the designation of a Cardinal when made by the Pope outside of a consistory has no legal effects. Consequently, if a person were to use physical violence on a Cardinal-designate, he would not thereby incur the penalties enacted against those who violate the personal immunity of a Cardinal.

Canon 2343, § 2, further indicates that the same penalties which are incurred by malicious strikers of Cardinals are incurred by malicious strikers of legates of the Roman Pontiff. Legates are certain ecclesiastical persons whom the Roman Pontiff sends to a particular province to take his place in the administration of ecclesiastical affairs.[41] There are three kinds of legates, namely, the *Legati a latere*, the *Legati nati* and the *Legati missi*. The *Legati a latere,* usually selected from the body of Cardinals, are those who are sent by the Pope to expedite some very urgent business or to represent the Pope in some great solemnity, v. g., to preside at a eucharistic congress. The second group of legates, the *Legati nati,* are bishops or archbishops who are ordinaries of certain sees which have a privilege whereby the one in charge of the see has the honorary title of legate. With regard to the *Legati nati* canon 270 clearly indicates that a bishop who on account of his see has the honorary title of apos-

40 Cappello, *De Censuris*, p. 251. Cf. canon 233.

41 Beste, *Introductio in Codicem*, p. 249.

tolic legate does not thereby acquire any special right. Finally, the *Legati missi* are titular archbishops who are sent to foreign countries as nuncios, internuncios, or apostolic delegates. Both the nuncios and the internuncios act as ambassadors from the Holy See in the country to which they are sent.[42] An apostolic delegate, however, is to perform a purely religious office, insofar as he is to watch over the condition of the Church in the country to which he is sent, and he is to remit reports to Rome on that issue.[43]

Patriarchs, who at one time in the Church's history were very important figures, do not possess any special jurisdictional power. They have, however, a certain prerogative of honor, and precedence according to the norms of canon 290.[44] Inasmuch as patriarchs do not enjoy any special rights by reason of their office, as far as the privilege of the canon is concerned they are put on a par with bishops and archbishops. Consequently, anyone who violates the personal immunity of patriarchs by assaulting or attacking them becomes guilty of the same crime and is punished with the same penalty as if he had violated the personal immunity of a bishop or of an archbishop.[45]

Concerning archbishops little comment for the immediate discussion need be offered other than to note that they are *usually* at the head of an ecclesiastical province and thus have suffragan bishops dependent on them. In this case they are called by the special name of metropolitans. There are, however, archbishops who are such only by title, and some also who are ordinaries of dioceses but have no suffragan bishops subject to them. All archbishops are included under the term "*archiepiscopus*" as used in canon 2343, § 3.[46]

A *latae sententiae* excommunication for which absolution is

42 An internuncio has the same powers and privileges as a nuncio, but not the same dignity. Internuncios are accredited by the Holy See to Holland, to Luxembourg and to most of the Central American countries.

43 Wernz-Vidal, *Ius de Personis*, n. 515. Cf. canons 265-270.

44 Cf. canon 271.

45 Cf. Wernz-Vidal, *Ius de Personis*, n. 517; Vermeersch-Creusen, *Epitome*, III, n. 542.

46 Blat, *Commentarium*, V, 237.

reserved *speciali modo* to the Holy See is also enacted against those who lay violent hands on the person of a bishop, whether residential or merely titular. This special immunity is granted to bishops, not because of their episcopal jurisdiction, but rather because of their episcopal consecration. For this reason the censure established in canon 2343, § 3, insofar as it applies to the case of physical injury inflicted on bishops, is not incurred until the priest has been consecrated a bishop. If a person should strike a bishop-elect, the excommunication incurred thereby would be reserved to the ordinary, not to the Holy See.[47]

B. *Vindicative Penalties for Assault upon Cardinals and Legates*

A person who maliciously strikes a Cardinal or a legate of the Roman Pontiff incurs, in addition to the excommunication, the penalty of legal infamy. This penalty is incurred *ipso facto,* and therefore no judicial sentence is required. The effects of legal infamy have been sufficiently discussed in connection with the vindicative penalties attaching to the violation of the Pope's personal immunity from real injury.

Besides the penalty of legal infamy a person who lays violent hands on the person of a Cardinal or of a legate of the Roman Pontiff is to be deprived of any benefices, offices, dignities, pensions, and any other charge which he may have in the Church. Blat, in commenting on this canon, observes that the legislator here used these terms in the plural number to indicate that the deprivation is to include *all* benefices, offices, dignities, pensions, and charges.[48] This penalty which entails the deprivation of benefices, offices, dignities, pensions and charges held by the culprit, is a *ferendae sententiae* penalty, and must therefore be inflicted by a judge or a superior.

Article 3 — Malicious Assault upon Other Clerics and Religious of Either Sex

Canon 2343, § 4: Qui in personam aliorum clericorum vel utriusque sexus religiosorum [*violentas manus iniecerit*], *subia-*

[47] Cappello, *De Censuris,* p. 251.

[48] *Commentarium,* V, 237.

ceat ipso facto excommunicationi Ordinario proprio reservatae, qui praeterea aliis poenis, si res ferat, pro suo prudenti arbitrio eum puniat.

A. The Censure of Excommunication

Canon 2343 follows a systematic gradation of persons, and in accordance with this gradation establishes correspondingly proportionate penalties for malicious assaults upon these persons. After enumerating the penalties for the violation of the personal immunity of members of the superior hierarchical ranks, the canon indicates the penalty for violations of the personal immunity of religious of either sex and of clerics who are not members of the previously mentioned hierarchical ranks. Violations of the privilege of the canon perpetrated against clerics who are not mentioned in the preceding sections of the canon, and also against religious, whether men or women, who enjoy the privilege of the canon, are punished with excommunication for which absolution is to be obtained from the proper ordinary of the delinquent. Although canon 2343 states that this excommunication is reserved to the *proper* ordinary, any ordinary can grant absolution from this penalty in occult cases.[49] If a bishop has given the priests of his diocese habitual faculties to grant absolution from censures reserved to the ordinary by law, then any priest with these faculties can absolve the excommunication incurred in consequence of the penal enactment of canon 2343, § 4.[50]

B. The Indeterminate Penalty

In cases in which the excommunication incurred through a violation of the privilege of the canon is reserved to the ordinary, the law grants to the same ordinary the power to inflict other penalties if in his discretion he deems them necessary. In most occurrences of this crime there will be some scandal, and the ordinary can therefore impose an appropriate penalty as reparation for the scandal which has been caused by the com-

49 Canon 2237, § 2.

50 Canon 199, § 1.

mission of the crime. This penalty, then, will have the effect of deterring others from the commission of a similar crime.[51]

The penalties which in his judgment the ordinary can inflict are not determined in the Code, nor has this point been elucidated by the canonical writers on penal law. Most of these writers are mainly concerned with a discussion of the excommunication enacted against the *percussores clericorum*, and dismiss the discussion of the vindicative penalties with a mere restatement of the canon.

Concerning the clause, "*qui praeterea aliis poenis, si res ferat, pro suo prudenti arbitrio eum puniat,*" Blat observes that the legislator has indeed established an indeterminate penalty, but that the words of the canon are preceptive in their juridical import.[52] Woywod (1880-1941), in translating this canon also seemed Woywod (1880-1941), in translating this canon also seemed to be of the opinion that the ordinary *must* inflict other penalties in cases reserved to him for absolution, for he stated that the proper ordinary *shall* moreover punish culprits with other appropriate penalties in his discretion.[53]

It is perhaps more accurate to say that the additional penalties can be inflicted only if some special gravity attends the case, i. e., *si res ferat*. In other words, if there be no special reason for the infliction of additional penalties, then the ordinary has no option to inflict them. On the other hand if there be a special reason for the infliction of additional penalties, then the ordinary must invoke some additional penalty. Accordingly, the word "*puniat*" must be considered as preceptive, but the phrase "*pro suo prudenti arbitrio*" must be considered as one containing facultative terms. The penalty is, therefore, preceptive *quoad existentiam*, but facultative (optional) *quoad speciem*.

Before the ordinary inflicts the penalty there are many factors which must influence his judgment. He must take into account the scandal that may have been given and the injury that may have been caused by the commission of the crime. Due

51 Sole, *De Delictis et Poenis*, p. 298.

52 *Commentarium*, V, 238. Cf. canon 2216, § 1, 1°.

53 *A Practical Commentary on the Code of Canon Law*, II, 495.

attention must be given to the age, the instruction, the education, the sex, and the state of the mind of the delinquent as well as to any circumstances which may alter the imputability of the crime.[54] In decreeing this additional penalty a very decisive factor for the ordinary in making his decision will be the state of life of the delinquent. An ordinary, for instance, may inflict severer penalties on clerics guilty of this crime than on lay persons, if the circumstances demand it.

One difficulty in this matter is the determination of the penalties which the ordinary may inflict. Inasmuch as canon 2343, § 4, leaves the specific determination of the penalties to the prudent judgment of the ordinary, it may be noted that he may apply any of the penances listed in canon 2313. These penances are imposed in the external forum, primarily for a vindicatory purpose, such as, v. g., the reparation of scandal.[55]

Canon 2313 lists the following as the principal penances that may be imposed:

1. The recitation of certain prayers;
2. Pious pilgrimages or other works of piety;
3. A special fast;
4. Alms for pious purposes;
5. A retreat for some days in a religious house.

The canon lists the foregoing as the *principal* penances, and it can therefore be concluded that the list is not to be considered as exclusive of others. A great latitude is given to the ordinary in canon 2343, § 4, in his choice of an appropriate penalty. Whereas it may be suggested that the ordinary inflict one of these penances, nonetheless he may inflict any other penalty which he considers proportionate to the offense. Since canon 2343, § 4, refers to the infliction of additional *poenae*, the ordinary is not restricted to the infliction of penances. As punishment for this crime the ordinary may inflict some of the vindicative penalties mentioned in canon 2291, such as, v. g., the imposition of a fine. If the culprit be a cleric, the ordinary may apply some of the penalties mentioned in canon 2298.

54 Canon 2218, § 1.

55 Ayrinhac, *Penal Legislation in the New Code of Canon Law*, p. 140.

CONCLUSIONS

As a result of this study the following conclusions are offered:

1. Until the ninth century, when particular ecclesiastical legislation was made for the first time for the protection of the clergy, civil laws protected the clergy against assaults. (P. 11.)

2. The fifteenth canon of the II General Council of the Lateran (1139), in which is contained mention of the privilege of the canon, was always considered as enacting a *latae sententiae* penalty. (Pp. 23-26.)

3. This canonical institute underwent no change during the period which runs from the time immediately prior to the Council of Trent to the publication of the present Code of Canon Law. (P. 36.)

4. In consequence of the privilege of the canon clerics are forbidden voluntarily to submit to injuries or to humiliating assaults, even for the sake of compensating a previous injury, but they are not forbidden by it to engage in field games, boxing matches and prize-fights, or to submit to hazing which is often required as a ceremony of initiation before candidates are admitted into fraternities, lodges, etc. Prize-fighting, however, is forbidden to clerics for the reason that it is an occupation which is unbecoming to the clerical state. (Pp. 58-61.)

5. From time to time the Holy See has expressly stated that priests belonging to one or the other of the various Oriental rites enjoy the privilege of the canon. In this study it was indicated that all Oriental clerics enjoy this privilege, even though the Holy See has not specifically declared so in an explicit manner. Not all Oriental clerics, however, enjoy the privilege as protected through canonical penalties to be incurred by the violators of the privilege. (Pp. 72-73.)

6. Cappello's opinion that malicious strikers of novices or quasi-religious do not incur the excommunication mentioned in canon 2343, § 4, is the safer one in practice. In the present study it was indicated that the act of striking a novice or a quasi-

religious constitutes a *delictum* according to the definition given in canon 2195. This crime, however, is not punished according to the norms of canon 2343, § 4, but rather according to the norms of canon 2325. (Pp. 81-84; 87.)

7. A subject of the Latin rite who maliciously strikes a cleric or a religious of an Oriental rite incurs the penalties mentioned in canon 2343. Subjects of the Oriental rites are liable to the excommunication incurred through malicious assaults upon the Pope, but they are not subject to the other provisions of canon 2343. (Pp. 97-98.)

8. The Code of Canon Law contains not only the first censure in universal law but also the first vindicative penalties to be incurred specifically through a malicious assault upon the Supreme Pontiff. (Pp. 114-115.)

9. When the excommunication which is incurred through a violation of the privilege of the canon is reserved to the ordinary, the law grants to the same ordinary power to inflict other penalties if in his discretion he deems them necessary. The terms of the canon which grants this power to ordinaries are preceptive if some special gravity attends the case; but the terms are facultative with regard to the species of the penalty that the ordinary may inflict. (Pp. 123-124.)

10. In inflicting an indeterminate penalty the ordinary not only may apply the penances of which mention is made in canon 2312, but he may also apply one or the other of the vindicative penalties mentioned in canons 2291 and 2298, applicable respectively to the cases in which the delinquents are of lay or clerical status. (P. 125.)

BIBLIOGRAPHY

Sources

Acta Apostolicae Sedis, Commentarium Officiale, Romae, 1909-1929; Civitate Vaticana, 1929 —.

Acta Sanctae Sedis, 41 vols., Romae, 1865-1908.

Canones et Decreta Sacrosancti Oecumenici Concilii Tridentini, Romae: ex Typographia Polyglotta A. C. de Propaganda Fide, 1882.

Codex Iuris Canonici Pii X Pontificis Maximi iussu digestus Benedicti XV auctoritate promulgatus, Romae: Typis Polyglottis Vaticanis, 1917.

Codicis Iuris Canonici Fontes, cura Emi Petri Card. Gasparri editi, 9 vols., Romae (postea Civitate Vaticana): Typis Polyglottis Vaticanis, 1923-1939. (Vols. VII-IX, ed. cura et studio Emi Iustiniani Card. Serédi.)

Codicis Dn. Iustiniani Sacratissimi Principis ex Repetita Praelectione Libri Novem Priores, Lugduni, 1553.

Codificazione Canonica Orientale, Fonti, Sacra Congregazione Orientale, Parte I, 16 vols., Parte II, 3 Serii, Città del Vaticano: Tipographia Poliglotta Vaticana, 1930 —.

Corpus Iuris Canonici, ed. Lipsiensis secunda post Aemilii Ludovici Richteri curas instruxit Aemilius Friedberg, 2 vols., Lipsiae: Ex Officina Bernhardi Tauchnitz, 1879-1881. Editio anastatice repetita, Lipsiae: Tauchnitz, 1922.

Corpus Iuris Civilis, Vol. II, *Codex Iustinianus,* quem recognovit et retractavit Paulus Krueger, ed. stereotypa nona, Berolini: Apud Weidmannos, 1915.

Corpus Iuris Civilis, Vol. III, *Novellae,* quas recognovit Rudolfus Schoell, absolvit Guglielmus Kroll, ed. stereotypa quinta, Berolini: Apud Weidmannos, 1928.

Decretales D. Gregorii Papae IX suae integritati una cum glossis restitutae, cum privilegio Gregorii XIII, Pont. Max., et aliorum Principum, Romae, 1582.

Decretum Gratiani emendatum et notationibus illustratum una cum glossis, Gregorii XIII, Pont. Max., iussu editum, 2 vols., Romae, 1582.

Jaffé, P., *Regesta Pontificum Romanorum ab condita Ecclesia ad annum post Christum natum MCXCVIII,* 2. ed., cura Wattenbach, Kaltenbrunner, Ewald, Loewenfeld, 2 vols. in 1, Lipsiae, 188g-1888.

Liber Sextus Decretalium D. Bonifacii Papae VIII suae integritati una cum Clementinis et Extravagantibus earumque Glossis restitutis, Romae, 1582.

Mansi, Ioannes, *Sacrorum Conciliorum Nova et Amplissima Collectio,* 53 vols. in 60, Parisiis, 1901-1927.

Monumenta Germaniae Historica, Legum Sectio I, *Leges Nationum Germanicarum,* tom. V, pars I, ed. Rudolph Sohm, Hannoverae, 1883.

Monumenta Germaniae Historica, Legum Sectio I, *Leges Nationum Germanicarum*, tom. V, pars II, ed. Ernest de Schwind, Hannoverae, 1926.

Monumenta Germaniae Historica, Legum Sectio II, *Capitularia Regum Francorum*, tom. I, ed. A. Boretius, Hannoverae, 1883.

Potthast, A., *Regesta Pontificum Romanorum inde ab anno post Christum natum MCXCVIII ad annum MCCCIV*, 2 vols., Berolini, 1874-1875.

Schroeder, H. J., *Canons and Decrees of the Council of Trent, Original Text with English Translation*, St. Louis: Herder Book Co., 1941.

Reference Works

Aertnys, Jos. - Damen, C. A., *Theologia Moralis*, 13. ed. (5. ed. post Codicem), 2 vols., Taurini-Romae: Marietti, 1939.

Aichner, Simon, *Compendium Juris Ecclesiastici*, 6. ed., Brixinae, 1887.

Albers, Pierre, *Manuel d'Histoire Ecclésiastique*, adaption de la seconde édition Hollandaise par René Hedde, 2 vols., Paris: Gabalda, 1923.

Alphonsus Marie de Ligoria, St., *Theologia Moralis*, cura et studio Leonardi Gaudé, 4 vols., Romae, 1905-1912.

Augustine, Charles, *A Commentary on the New Code of Canon Law*, 8 vols., St. Louis: Herder Book Co., 1925-1938. Vol. I, 6. ed., 1931; Vol. II, 6. ed., 1936; Vol. III, 5. ed., 1938; Vol. IV, 3. ed., 1925; Vol. V, 5. ed., 1935; Vol. VI, 3. ed., 1931; Vol. VII, 3. ed., 1930; Vol. VIII, 3. ed., 1931.

Ayrinhac, H. A. - Lydon, P. J., *Penal Legislation in the New Code of Canon Law*, revised edition, New York: Benziger, 1936.

Barbosa, Augustinus, *Pastoralis Solicitudinis sive de Officio et Potestate Episcopi Descriptio*, 3 vols. in 1, Lugduni, 1656.

Benedictus XIV, *De Synodo Dioecesana*, 2 vols., Romae, 1806.

Berardi, Carolus S., *Gratiani Canones Genuini ab Apocryphis Discreti*, 2. ed. Veneta, 3 vols. in 4, Venetiis, 1783.

Bernardus Papiensis, *Summa Decretalium*, ed. E. A. T. Laspeyres, Ratisbonae, 1860.

Berutti, Christophorus, *Institutiones Iuris Canonici*, 6 vols., Vol. III, Taurini-Romae: Marietti, 1936.

Beste, Udalricus, *Introductio in Codicem*, ed. altera, Collegeville, Minn.: St. John's Abbey Press, 1944.

Blat, Albertus, *Commentarium Textus Codicis Iuris Canonici*, 5 vols. in 6, Romae: Ex Typographia Pontificia in Instituto Pii IX, 1919-1927.

Cambridge Medieval History, The, 8 vols., New York: Macmillan, 1911-1936. Vol. V, edited by J. R. Tanner, C. W. Previté-Orton and Z. N. Brooke.

Cappello, Felix, *De Censuris iuxta Codicem Iuris Canonici*, 2. ed., Taurinorum Augustae: Marietti, 1925.

——, *Institutiones Iuris Publici Ecclesiastici*, 2 vols., Augustae Taurinorum: Marietti, 1907.

——, *Summa Iuris Canonici*, 3 vols., Vol. I, 3. ed., Romae: Apud Aedes Universitatis Gregorianae, 1938.

——, *Tractatus Canonico-Moralis de Sacramentis*, 3 vols. in 6, Taurinorum Augustae: Marietti, 1932-1939. Vol. II, Pars II, 1935.

Catholic Encyclopoedia, The, 15 vols., Index, and 2 Supplements, New York, 1907-1922.

Cavigioli, Ioannes, *De Censuris Latae Sententiae quae in Codice Iuris Canonici Continentur Commentariolum*, Torino: Libraria Editrice Internazionale, 1919.

Cerato, Prosdocimus, *Censurae Vigentes Ipso Facto a Codice Iuris Canonici Excerptae*, 2. ed., Patavii: Typis Seminarii, 1921.

Chelodi, Ioannes, *Ius Poenale et Ordo Procedendi in Iudiciis Criminalibus iuxta Codicem Iuris Canonici*, Tridenti: Libr. Edit. Tridentum, 1925 [1920!].

——, *Ius de Personis iuxta Codicem Iuris Canonici*, ed. altera a Sac. Ernesto Bertagnolli recognita et aucta, Tridenti: Libr. Edit. Tridentum, 1927.

Cicognani, Amleto Giovanni, *Canon Law*, authorized English version by J. O'Hara and F. Brennan, 2. revised ed., Philadelphia: Dolphin Press, 1935.

Cipollini, Albertus D., *De Censuris Latae Sententiae iuxta Codicem Iuris Canonici*, Taurini: Marietti, 1925.

Cocchi, Guidus, *Commentarium in Codicem Iuris Canonici*, 8 vols. in 5, Taurinorum Augustae: Marietti, 1930-1940. Lib. II, Pars I, 3. ed., 1930; Lib. II, Pars II, 3. ed., 1932.

Coronata, Mattheus Conte a, *Institutiones Iuris Canonici ad Usum Utriusque Cleri et Scholarum*, 5 vols., Romae: Marietti, 1933-1939. Vols. I et II, 2. ed., 1939; Vol. III, 1933; Vol. IV, 1935; Vol. V, 1936.

——, *Jus Publicum Ecclesiasticum*, 2. ed., Taurini: Marietti, 1934.

Daoyz, Stephanus, *Juris Pontificii Tomus IV in duas partes divisus*, 2 vols., Burdigalae, 1624.

De Clercq, Carlo, *La Legislation Religieuse Franque de Clovis à Charlemagne* (507-814), Louvain: Bureaux du Recueil Bibliothèque de l'Université: Paris: Librairie du Recueil Sirey S. A., 1936.

De Meester, Alphonsus, *Juris Canonici et Juris Canonico-Civilis Compendium*, ed. nova, 3 vols. in 4, Brugis: Desclée, De Brouwer, 1921-1928.

Devoti, Ioannes, *Jus Canonicum Universum Publicum et Privatum*, 3 vols., Romae, 1837.

Dictionnaire de Théologie Catholique, 14 vols., Paris: Librairie Letouzey et Ané, 1903-1939.

Dictionnaire Pratique des Connaissances Religieuses, 6 vols., Paris: Librairie Letouzey et Ané, 1925-1928.

Downs, John E., *The Concept of Clerical Immunity*, The Catholic University of America Canon Law Studies, n. 126, Washington, D. C.: The Catholic University of America Press, 1941.

Duchesne, Louis, *Christian Worship: Its Origin and Evolution,* translated by M. L. McClure, New York and London, 1903.

Eichmann, Eduardus, *Das Strafrecht des Codex Iuris Canonici,* Paderborn: Schöningh, 1920.

Ernout, A. - Meillet, A., *Dictionnaire Étymologique de la Langue Latine,* Paris: Librairie C. Klinchsieck, 1932.

Fagnanus, Prosper, *Commentaria in Quinque Libros Decretalium,* 5 vols. in 3, Venetiis, 1709-1729.

Fanfani, Ludovicus, *De Iure Religiosorum,* 2. ed., Taurini-Romae: Marietti, 1925.

Ferraris, Lucius, *Prompta Bibliotheca Canonica, Juridica, Moralis, Theologica, necnon Ascetica, Polemica, Rubricistica, Historica,* 8 vols., Romae, 1885-1892. Vol. IX ed. I. Bucceroni, Romae, 1899.

Ferreres, Ioannes, *Institutiones Canonicae,* 2. ed., 2 vols., Barcinone: Subirana, 1920.

Findlay, Stephen William, *Canonical Norms Governing the Deposition and Degradation of Clerics,* The Catholic University of America Canon Law Studies, n. 130, Washington, D. C.: The Catholic University of America Press, 1941.

Funk, Francis Xavier, *Manual of Church History,* translated from the German by P. Perciballi and edited by W. H. Kent, 2 vols., London: Burns, Oates and Washbourne, Ltd., 1938.

Genicot, Eduardus - Salsman, I., *Institutiones Theologiae Moralis,* 13. ed., 2 vols., Bruxellis: L'Édition Universelle, 1936.

Gignac, Joseph N., *Compendium Juris Canonici,* 2 vols., Québec, 1901-1903.

Gonzalez-Tellez, Emmanuel, *Commentaria Perpetua in Singulos Textus Quinque Librorum Decretalium Gregorii IX,* 5 vols., Venetiis, 1756.

Grandclaude, E., *Jus Canonicum,* 3 vols., Parisiis, 1882-1883.

Gross, Carl, *Lehrbuch des katholischen Kirchenrechts,* 4. ed., Wien, 1903.

Hefele, Carl - Leclercq, Henri, *Histoire des Conciles,* 10 vols. in 19, Paris: Librairie Letouzey et Ané, 1907-1938.

Heylen, V., *De Censuris,* 4. ed., Mechliniae: H. Dessain, 1945.

Hinschius, Paul, *Das Kirchenrecht der Katholiken und Protestanten in Deutschland,* 6 vols., Berlin, 1869-1897.

Hollweck, Joseph, *Die kirchlichen Strafgesetze,* Mainz, 1899.

Hostiensis, Cardinalis (Henricus de Segusio), *Summa Aurea,* Venetiis, 1570.

Kober, F., *Der Kirchenbann nach den Grundsätzen des canonischen Rechts,* Tübingen, 1863.

Kuttner, Stephan, *Kanonistische Schuldlehre von Gratian bis auf die Dekretalen Gregors IX,* Città del Vaticano: Biblioteca Apostolica Vaticana, 1935.

Leage, R. W., *Roman Private Law,* 2. ed. by C. H. Ziegler, London: Macmillan, 1942.

Lega, Michael, *Praelectiones in Textum Iuris Canonici — De Delictis et Poenis,* 2. ed., Romae, 1910.

Leonhard, Rudolph, *Institutionen des römischen Rechts,* Leipzig, 1894.

Lijdsman, Bernard, *Introductio in Jus Canonicum,* 2 vols., Hilversum in Hollandia: Sumptibus Societatis Editricis Pontificiae Anonymae, 1924-1929.

McNeill, John J. - Gamer, Helena M., *Medieval Handbooks of Penance,* a translation of the principal *libri poenitentiales* and selections from related documents, New York: Columbia University Press, 1938. This work is n. XXIX of the series: *Records of Civilization, Sources and Studies,* edited under the auspices of the Department of History, Columbia University.

Maroto, Philippus, *Institutiones Iuris Canonici ad Normam Novi Codicis,* 2 vols., Vol. I, Romae: Matriti, 1919.

Maupied, Franciscus, L. M., *Juris Canonici Universi per Faciliorem Methodum ad Veram Praxim Sincere Redacti Compendium,* 2 vols., Lutetiae Parisiorum, 1863.

Michiels, Gommarus, *Normae Generales Iuris Canonici,* 2 vols., Lublin: Universitas Catholica, 1929.

Moriarity, Francis E., *The Extraordinary Absolution from Censures,* The Catholic University of America Canon Law Studies, n. 113, Washington, D. C.: The Catholic University of America, 1938.

Mosheim, John L., *An Ecclesiastical History, Ancient and Modern,* translated from the Latin by Archibald Maclaine, 6 vols., London, 1825.

Mothon, Joseph, *Institutions Canoniques a l'usage des Curies Episcopales, du Clergé Paroissial, et des Familles Religieuses,* 3 vols., Brugis: Desclée, De Brouwer, 1922-1924.

Mourret, Fernand, *A History of the Catholic Church,* translated by Newton Thompson, 6 vols., St. Louis and London: Herder Book Co., 1930-1946.

Müller, Michael, *Ethik und Recht in der Lehre von der Verantwortlichkeit,* Regensburg: Habbel, 1932.

Noldin, H. - Schönegger, A., *De Censuris,* Oeniponte: Typis et Sumptibus Fel. Rauch, 1923.

Ojetti, B., *Commentarium in Codicem Iuris Canonici,* 4 vols., Romae: Apud Aedes Universitatis Gregorianae, 1927-1931.

O'Leary, Charles G., *Religious Dismissed after Perpetual Profession,* The Catholic University of America Canon Law Studies, n. 184, Washington, D. C.: The Catholic University of America Press, 1943.

O'Neill, Francis J., *The Dismissal of Religious in Temporary Vows,* The Catholic University of America Canon Law Studies, n. 166, Washington, D. C.: The Catholic University of America Press, 1942.

Panormitanus, Abbas (Nicolaus de Tudeschis), *Commentaria in Quinque Libros Decretalium,* 5 vols. in 7, Venetiis, 1588.

Phillips, Georg, *Kirchenrecht*, 7 vols., Regensburg, 1845-1872; Vol. VIII, 1, by F. Vering, Regensburg, 1889.

Pighi, J. B., *Censurae Sententiae Latae et Irregularitates quas habet "Codex Iuris Canonici,"* 7. ed., Verona: Cinquetti, 1922.

Pirhing, Enricus, *Jus Canonicum Nova Methodo Explicatum*, 5 vols. in 3, Dilingae, 1722.

Piscetta, A. - Gennaro, A., *Elementa Theologiae Moralis*, 7 vols., Vol. IV, 2. ed., Torino: Editrice Internazionale, 1929.

Pistocchi, Mario, *I Canoni Penali de Codice Ecclesiastico*, Torino-Roma: Marietti, 1925.

Plöchl, Willibald, *Das Eherecht des Magisters Gratianus*, Leipzig und Wien: Franz Deuticke, 1935.

Pollock, Frederick - Maitland, Frederick, *History of English Law before the Time of Edward I*, 2. ed., 2 vols., Cambridge, 1899.

Poulet, Charles, *A History of the Catholic Church*, authorized translation and adaption from the fourth French edition by Sidney Raemers, 2 vols., St. Louis and London: Herder Book Co., 1941-1943.

Prümmer, Dominicus, *Manuale Theologiae Moralis*, 8. ed., recognita a E. M. Münch, 3 vols., Friburgi Brisgoviae: Herder Book Co., 1935-1936.

Raus, J. B., *Institutiones Canonicae*, 2. ed., Lugduni-Parisiis: Typis Emmanuelis Vitte, 1931.

Regatillo, Eduardus, *Institutiones Iuris Canonici*, 2 vols., Santander: Sal Terrae, 1941-1942.

Reiffenstuel, Anacletus, *Jus Canonicum Universum*, 5 vols. in 7, Parisiis, 1864-1870.

Richter, Aemilius L., *Lehrbuch des katholischen und evangelischen Kirchenrechts*, 8. ed. by R. Dove and W. Kahl, 1 vol. in 2, Leipzig, 1886.

Riesner, Albert J., *Apostates and Fugitives from Religious Institutes*, The Catholic University of America Canon Law Studies, n. 168, Washington, D. C.: The Catholic University of America Press, 1942.

Roelker, Edward, *Principles of Privilege according to the Code of Canon Law*, The Catholic University of America Canon Law Studies, n. 35, Washington, D. C.: The Catholic University of America, 1926.

Rufinus, *Summa Decretorum*, ed. H. Singer, Paderborn, 1902.

Sägmüller, Johannes B., *Lehrbuch des katholischen Kirchenrechts*, 2 vols., Freiburg im Breisgau, 1900-1904. Vol. I, 4. ed. (1. ed. post Codicem) was issued in 4 installments which appeared in 1925, 1926, 1930 and 1934 respectively.

Salucci, Raffaele, *Il Diritto Penale*, 2 vols., Subiaco: Tipografia dei Monasteri, 1926-1930.

Salvagio, Iulius Laurentius, *Antiquitatum Christianarum Institutiones*, 6 vols., Venetiis, 1794.

Sanguinetti, Sebastianus, *Institutiones Iuris Ecclesiastici Privati*, Romae, 1884.

Santi, Franciscus, *Praelectiones Juris Canonici*, 4. ed., 5 vols. in 3, a Martino Leitner, Ratisbonae-Romae, 1903-1905.

Schaefer (Schäfer), Timotheus, *De Religiosis ad Normam Codicis Iuris Canonici*, 3. ed., Romae: Typis Polyglottis Vaticanis, 1940.

Schaff, Philip, *History of the Christian Church*, 7 vols., Vol. V by David S. Schaff, New York, 1907.

Schmalzgrueber, Franciscus, *Jus Ecclesiasticum Universum*, 5 vols. in 12, Romae, 1843-1845.

Schmitz, Hermann Joseph, *Die Bussbücher und die Bussdisciplin der Kirche*, Mainz, 1883.

Schroeder, H. J., *Disciplinary Decrees of the General Councils*, Text, Translation and Commentary, London-St. Louis: Herder Book Co., 1937.

Scott, S. P., *The Civil Law*, 17 vols. in 7, Cincinnati: The Central Trust Co., 1932.

Sebastianelli, Gulielmus, *Praelectiones Juris Canonici*, Vol. I, *De Personis*, 2. ed., Romae, 1905.

Sipos, Stephanus, *Enchiridion Iuris Canonici*, Pécs: Ex Typographia "Haladás R. T.," 1926.

Sole, Iacobus, *De Delictis et Poenis*, Romae: Pustet, 1920.

Stutz, Ulrich, *Der Geist des Codex iuris canonici*, Kirchenrechtliche Abhandlungen hrsg. von Ulrich Stutz, 92. und 93. Heft, Stuttgart: Verlag von Ferdinand Enke, 1918.

Suarez, Franciscus, *Opera Omnia*, 28 vols., Parisiis, 1856-1878.

Sweeney, Francis P., *The Reduction of Clerics to the Lay State*, The Catholic University of America Canon Law Studies, n. 223, Washington, D. C.: The Catholic University of America Press, 1945.

Swoboda, Innocent R., *Ignorance in Relation to Imputability of Delicts*, The Catholic University of America Canon Law Studies, n. 143, Washington, D. C.: The Catholic University of America Press, 1941.

Thomas Aquinas, St., *Summa Theologica*, 6 vols., Taurini: Marietti, 1932.

——, *Omnia Opera*, 34 vols., Parisiis, 1871-1880.

Thomassinus, Ludovicus, *Vetus et Nova Ecclesiae Disciplina circa Beneficia et Beneficiarios*, 10 vols., Magontiaci, 1787.

Tixeront, J., *History of Dogmas*, 3 vols., translated from 5. French ed. by H. L. B., Vol. III, 2. ed., London and St. Louis, 1926.

Vermeersch, A. - Creusen, I., *Epitome Iuris Canonici*, 3 vols., Mechliniae-Romae: H. Dessain, 1934-1937. Vol. I, 6. ed., 1937; Vol. II, 5. ed., 1934; Vol. III, 5. ed., 1936.

Wernz, Franciscus, *Ius Decretalium*, 2. ed., 6 vols., Romae et Prati, 1906-1913.

——, - Vidal, Petrus, *Ius Canonicum*, 7 vols. in 8, Romae: Universitas Gregoriana, 1928-1943. Vol. I, 1938; Vol. II, 3. ed., a P. Philippo Aguirre recognita, 1943; Vol. III, 1933; Vol. IV, Pars I, 1934; Vol. IV, Pars I, 1935; Vol. V, 2. ed., 1928; Vol. VI, 1928; Vol. VII, 1937.

Woywod, Stanislaus, *A Practical Commentary on the Code of Canon Law*, 8. ed., revised by Callistus Smith, 2 vols., New York: Jos. F. Wagner, Inc., 1944.

Zitelli-Natali, Zephyrinus, *Epitome Historico-Canonica Conciliorum Generalium*, Romae, 1881.

Zollman, Carl, *American Church Law*, St. Paul: West Publishing Co., 1933.

Principal Articles

Anonymous, "Privilèges du clergé — *Analecta Juris Pontificii*, IV, Pars 2 (1866), 1789-2000.

Cappello, F., "Praescriptum can. 2343, § 4 seu excommunicatio lata in percussores clericorum et religiosorum" — *Jus Pontificium*, V (1926), 29-33.

Ciprotti, P., "De iniuria et diffamatione in iure poenali ecclesiastico" — *Apollinaris*, X (1937), 53-75; 233-268; 431-456.

——, "De consummatione delictorum attento eorum elemento obiectivo" — *Apollinaris*, VIII (1935), 224-248: 377-427; IX (1936), 404-414.

Fallon, M. J., "The Privilege of the Canon" — *Irish Ecclesiastical Review*, 5. series, LI (1938), 74-78.

Goyeneche, S., "Consultationes" — *CpR*, VII (1926), 186-190.

Herman, A., "De ritu in iure canonico" — *Orientalia Christiana*, XXXII (1933), 96-158.

Hüffer, H., "Das *Privilegium Canonis*" — *AKKR*, III (1858), 155-169.

Kuttner, S., "The Father of the Science of Canon Law" — *The Jurist*, I (1941), 3-19.

Ludwig, A., "Geschichte des Sacrilege nach den Quellen des katholischen Kirchenrechts" — *AKKR*, LXIX (1893), 169-252.

Roberti, F., "Adnotationes" — *Apollinaris*, VIII (1935), 30-31.

Teodori, I., "Privilegium canonis—Consultationes"—*Apollinaris*, V (1932), 112-116.

Periodicals

Analecta Juris Pontificii, Romae, 1855-1869; Parisiis, 1872-1891.

Apollinaris, Romae, 1928 —.

Archiv für katholisches Kirchenrecht, Innsbruck, 1857-1861; Mainz, 1862 —.

Catholic Review, The, Washington, D. C., 1936 —.

Commentarium pro Religiosis, Romae, 1920; ab anno 1935: *Commentarium pro Religiosis et Missionariis*.

Irish Ecclesiastical Record, The, Dublin, 1864.

Jurist, The, Washington, D. C.: The Catholic University of America, 1941 —.

Jus Pontificium, Romae, 1921.

Orientalia Christiana, Romae, 1923-1934.

ABBREVIATIONS

AKKR — *Archiv für katholisches Kirchenrecht.*
C. — Codex Iustinianus.
CpR — *Commentarium pro Religiosis.*
Fontes — *Codicis Iuris Canonici Fontes cura . . . Gasparri editi.*
Fonti — *Codificazione Canonica Orientale, Fonti.*
Jaffé — *Regesta Pontificum Romanorum* (edited by Ewald, Kaltenbrunner, Loewenfeld).
Mansi — *Sacrorum Conciliorum Nova et Amplissima Collectio.*
MGH — *Monumenta Germaniae historica.*
S. C. S. Off. — Suprema Congregatio Sancti Officii.

ALPHABETICAL INDEX

BIOGRAPHICAL NOTE

JAMES MCGRATH was born April 13, 1917, in Philadelphia, Pennsylvania. He attended St. Nicholas' Parochial School in Buffalo, New York, and Roman Catholic High School, in Philadelphia. In September of 1935 he was admitted to the Seminary of St. Charles Borromeo, Philadelphia, where he completed his course in Philosophy and Theology. There he received the degree of the Baccalaureate of Arts in 1939. He was ordained to the Sacred Priesthood on May 29, 1943. In the fall of that year he enrolled in the school of Canon Law of the Catholic University of America, where he received the degree of the Baccalaureate in Canon Law in May of 1944, and the degree of the Licentiate in Canon Law in May, 1945.

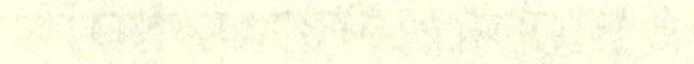

CANON LAW STUDIES*

1. FRERIKS, REV. CELESTINE A., C.PP.S., J.C.D., Religious Congregations in Their External Relations, 121 pp., 1916.
2. GALLIHER, REV. DANIEL M., O.P., J.C.D., Canonical Elections, 117 pp., 1917.
3. BORKOWSKI, REV. AURELIUS L., O.F.M., J.C.D., De Confraternitatibus Ecclesiasticis, 136 pp., 1918.
4. CASTILLO, REV. CAYO, J.C.D., Disertacion Historico-Canonica sobre la Potestad del Cabildo en Sede Vacante o Impedida del Vicario Capitular, 99 pp., 1919 (1918).
5. KUBELBECK, REV. WILLIAM J., S.T.B., J.C.D., The Sacred Penitentiaria and Its Relation to Faculties of Ordinaries and Priests, 129 pp., 1918.
6. PETROVITS, REV. JOSEPH, J.C., S.T.D., J.C.D., The New Church Law on Matrimony, X-461 pp., 1919.
7. HICKEY, REV. JOHN J., S.T.B., J.C.D., Irregularities and Simple Impediments in the New Code of Canon Law, 100 pp., 1920.
8. KLEKOTKA, REV. PETER J., S.T.B., J.C.D., Diocesan Consultors, 179 pp., 1920.
9. WANENMACHER, REV. FRANCIS, J.C.D., The Evidence in Ecclesiastical Procedure Affecting the Marriage Bond, 1920 (Printed 1935).
10. GOLDEN, REV. HENRY FRANCIS, J.C.D., Parochial Benefices in the New Code, IV-119 pp., 1921 (Printed 1925).
11. KOUDELKA, REV. CHARLES J., J.C.D., Pastors, Their Rights and Duties According to the New Code of Canon Law, 211 pp., 1921.
12. MELO, REV. ANTONIUS, O.F.M., J.C.D., De Exemptione Regularium, X-188 pp., 1921.
13. SCHAAF, REV. VALENTINE THEODORE, O.F.M., S.T.B., J.C.D., The Cloister, X-180 pp., 1921.
14. BURKE, REV. THOMAS JOSEPH, S.T.D., J.C.D., Competence in Ecclesiastical Tribunals, IV-117 pp., 1922.
15. LEECH, REV. GEORGE LEO, J.C.D., A Comparative Study of the Constitution "Apostolicae Sedis" and the "Codex Juris Canonici," 179 pp., 1922.
16. MOTRY, REV. HUBERT LOUIS, S.T.D., J.C.D., Diocesan Faculties According to the Code of Canon Law, II-167 pp., 1922.
17. MURPHY, REV. GEORGE LAWRENCE, J.C.D., Delinquencies and Penalties in the Administration and the Reception of the Sacraments, IV-121 pp., 1923.

* From nn. 1-100 inclusive only nn. 25 and 57 are still obtainable.
From n. 101 onward all numbers are available except the following: nn. 101-118 inclusive, and also n. 122.

18. O'Reilly, Rev. John Anthony, S.T.B., J.C.D., Ecclesiastical Sepulture in the New Code of Canon Law, II-129 pp., 1923.
19. Michalicka, Rev. Wenceslas Cyril, O.S.B., J.C.D., Judicial Procedure in Dismissal of Clerical Exempt Religious, 107 pp., 1923.
20. Dargin, Rev. Edward Vincent, S.T.B., J.C.D., Reserved Cases According to the Code of Canon Law, IV-103 pp., 1924.
21. Godfrey, Rev. John A., S.T.B., J.C.D., The Right of Patronage According to the Code of Canon Law, 153 pp., 1924.
22. Hagedorn, Rev. Francis Edward, J.C.D., General Legislation on Indulgences, II-154 pp., 1924.
23. King, Rev. James Ignatius, J.C.D., The Administration of the Sacraments to Dying Non-Catholics, V-141 pp., 1924.
24. Winslow, Rev. Francis Joseph, O.F.M., J.C.D., Vicars and Prefects Apostolic, IV-149 pp., 1924.
25. Correa, Rev. Jose Servelion, S.T.L., J.C.D., La Potestad Legislativa de la Iglesia Catolica, IV-127 pp., 1925.
26. Dugan, Rev. Henry Francis, A.M., J.C.D., The Judiciary Department of the Diocesan Curia, 87 pp., 1925.
27. Keller, Rev. Charles Frederick, S.T.B., J.C.D., Mass Stipends, 167 pp., 1925.
28. Paschang, Rev. John Linus, J.C.D., The Sacramentals According to the Code of Canon Law, 129 pp., 1925.
29. Piontek, Rev. Cyrillus, O.F.M., S.T.B., J.C.D., De Indulto Exclaustrationis necnon Saecularizationis, XIII-289 pp., 1925.
30. Kearney, Rev. Richard Joseph, S.T.B., J.C.D., Sponsors at Baptism According to the Code of Canon Law, IV-127 pp. 1925.
31. Bartlett, Rev. Chester Joseph, A.M., LL.B., J.C.D., The Tenure of Parochial Property in the United States of America, V-108 pp., 1926.
32. Kilker, Rev. Adrian Jerome, J.C.D., Extreme Unction, V-425 pp., 1926.
33. McCormick, Rev. Robert Emmet, J.C.D., Confessors of Religious, VIII-266 pp., 1926.
34. Miller, Rev. Newton Thomas, J.C.D., Founded Masses According to the Code of Canon Law, VII-93 pp., 1926.
35. Roelker, Rev. Edward G., S.T.D., J.C.D., Principles of Privilege According to the Code of Canon Law, XI-166 pp., 1926.
36. Bakalarczyk, Rev. Richardus, M.I.C., J.U.D., De Novitiatu, VIII-208 pp., 1927.
37. Pizzuti, Rev. Lawrence, O.F.M., J.U.L., De Parochis Religiosis, 1927. (Not Printed).
38. Bliley, Rev. Nicholas Martin, O.S.B., J.C.D., Altars According to the Code of Canon Law, XIX-132 pp., 1927.
39. Brown, Mr. Brendan Francis, A.B., LL.M., J.U.D., The Canonical

Juristic Personality with Special Reference to its Status in the United States of America, V-212 pp., 1927.

40. CAVANAUGH, REV. WILLIAM THOMAS, C.P., J.U.D., The Reservation of the Blessed Sacrament, VIII-101 pp., 1927.

41. DOHENY, REV. WILLIAM J., C.S.C., A.B., J.U.D., Church Property: Modes of Acquisition, X-118 pp., 1927.

42. FELDHAUS, REV. ALOYSIUS H., C.PP.S., J.C.D., Oratories, IX-141 pp., 1927.

43. KELLY, REV. JAMES PATRICK, A.B., J.C.D., The Jurisdiction of the Simple Confessor, X-208 pp., 1927.

44. NEUBERGER, REV. NICHOLAS J., J.C.D., Canon 6 or the Relation of the Codex Juris Canonici to the Preceding Legislation, V-95 pp., 1927.

45. O'KEEFE, REV. GERALD MICHAEL, J.C.D., Matrimonial Dispensations, Powers of Bishops, Priests, and Confessors, VIII-232 pp., 1927.

46. QUIGLEY, REV. JOSEPH A. M., A.B., J.C.D., Condemned Societies, 139 pp., 1927.

47. ZAPLOTNIK, REV. JOHANNES LEO, J.C.D., De Vicariis Foraneis, X-142 pp., 1927.

48. DUSKIE, REV. JOHN ALOYSIUS, A.B., J.C.D., The Canonical Status of the Orientals in the United States, VIII-196 pp., 1928.

49. HYLAND, REV. FRANCIS EDWARD, J.C.D., Excommunication, Its Nature, Historical Development and Effects, VIII-181 pp., 1928.

50. REINMANN, REV. GERALD JOSEPH, O.M.C., J.C.D., The Third Order Secular of Saint Francis, 201 pp., 1928.

51. SCHENK, REV. FRANCIS J., J.C.D., The Matrimonal Impediments of Mixed Religion and Disparity of Cult, XVI-318 pp., 1929.

52. COADY, REV. JOHN JOSEPH, S.T.D., J.U.D., A.M., The Appointment of Pastors, VIII-150 pp., 1929.

53. KAY, REV. THOMAS HENRY, J.C.D., Competence in Matrimonial Procedure, VIII-164 pp., 1929.

54. TURNER, REV. SIDNEY JOSEPH, C.P., J.U.D., The Vow of Poverty, XLIX-217 pp., 1929.

55. KEARNEY, REV. RAYMOND A., A.B., S.T.D., J.C.D., The Principles of Delegation, VII-149 pp., 1929.

56. CONRAN, REV. EDWARD JAMES, A.B., J.C.D., The Interdict, V-163 pp., 1930.

57. O'NEIL, REV. WILLIAM H., J.C.D., Papal Rescripts of Favor, VII-218 pp., 1930.

58. BASTNAGEL, REV. CLEMENT VINCENT, J.U.D., The Appointment of Parochial Adjutants and Assistants, XV-257 pp., 1930.

59. FERRY, REV. WILLIAM A., A.B., J.C.D., Stole Fees, V-136 pp., 1930.

60. COSTELLO, REV. JOHN MICHAEL, A.B., J.C.D., Domicile and Quasi-Domicile, VII-201 pp., 1930.

61. KREMER, REV. MICHAEL NICHOLAS, A.B., S.T.B., J.C.D., Church Support in the United States, VI-136 pp., 1930.
62. ANGULA, REV. LUIS, C.M., J.C.D., Legislation de la Iglesia sobre la intencion en la application de la Santa Misa, VII-104 pp., 1931.
63. FREY, REV. WOLFGANG NORBERT, O.S.B., A.B., J.C.D., The Act of Religious Profession, VIII-174 pp., 1931.
64. ROBERTS, REV. JAMES BRENDAN, A.B., J.C.D., The Banns of Marriage, XIV-140 pp., 1931.
65. RYDER, REV. RAYMOND ALOYSIUS, A.B., J.C.D., Simony, IX-151 pp., 1931.
66. CAMPAGNA, REV. ANGELO, PH.D., J.U.D., Il Vicario Generale del Vescovo, VII-205 pp., 1931.
67. COX, REV. JOSEPH GODFREY, A.B., J.C.D., The Administration of Seminaries, VI-124 pp., 1931.
68. GREGORY, REV. DONALD J., J.U.D., The Pauline Privilege, XV-165 pp., 1931.
69. DONOHUE, REV. JOHN F., J.C.D., The Impediment of Crime, VII-110 pp., 1931.
70. DOOLEY, REV. EUGENE A., O.M.I., J.C.D., Church Law on Sacred Relics, IX-143 pp., 1931.
71. ORTH, REV. CLEMENT RAYMOND, O.M.C., J.C.D., The Approbation of Religious Institutes, 171 pp., 1931.
72. PERNICONE, REV. JOSEPH M., A.B., J.C.D., The Ecclesiastical Prohibition of Books, XII-267 pp., 1932.
73. CLINTON, REV. CONNELL, A.B., J.C.D., The Paschal Precept, IX-108 pp., 1932.
74. DONNELLY, REV. FRANCIS B., A.M., S.T.L., J.C.D., The Diocesan Synod, VIII-125 pp., 1932.
75. TORRENTE, REV. CAMILO, C.M.F., J.C.D., Las Processiones Sagradas, V-145 pp., 1932.
76. MURPHY, REV. EDWIN J., C.PP.S., J.C.D., Suspension Ex Informata Conscientia, XI-122 pp., 1932.
77. MACKENZIE, REV. ERIC F., A.M., S.T.L., J.C.D., The Delict of Heresy in its Commission, Penalization, Absolution, VII-124 pp., 1932.
78. LYONS, REV. AVITUS E., S.T.B., J.C.D., The Collegiate Tribunal of First Instance, XI-147 pp., 1932.
79. CONNOLLY, REV. THOMAS A., J.C.D., Appeals, XI-195 pp., 1932.
80. SANGMEISTER, REV. JOSEPH V., A.B., J.C.D., Force and Fear as Precluding Matrimonial Consent, V-211 pp., 1932.
81. JAEGER, REV. LEO A., A.B., J.C.D., The Administration of Vacant and Quasi-Vacant Episcopal Sees in the United States, IX-229 pp., 1932.
82. RIMLINGER, REV. HERBERT T., J.C.D., Error Invalidating Matrimonial Consent, VII-79 pp., 1932.

83. BARRETT, REV. JOHN D. M., S.S., J.C.D., A Comparative Study of the Third Plenary Council of Baltimore and the Code, IX-221 pp., 1932.
84. CARBERRY, REV. JOHN J., PHD., S.T.D., J.C.D., The Juridical Form of Marriage, X-177 pp., 1934.
85. DOLAN, REV. JOHN L., A.B., J.C.D., The Defensor Vinculi, XII-157 pp., 1934.
86. HANNAN, REV. JEROME D., A.M., S.T.D., LL.B., J.C.D., The Canon Law of Wills, IX-517 pp., 1934.
87. LEMIEUX, REV. DELISE A., A.M., J.C.D., The Sentence in Ecclesiastical Procedure, IX-131 pp., 1934.
88. O'ROURKE, REV. JAMES J., A.B., J.C.D., Parish Registers, VII-109 pp., 1934.
89. TIMLIN, REV. BARTHOLOMEW, O.F.M., A.M., J.C.D., Conditional Matrimonial Consent, X-381 pp., 1934.
90. WAHL, REV. FRANCIS X., A.B., J.C.D., The Matrimonial Impediments of Consanguinity and Affinity, VI-125 pp., 1934.
91. WHITE, REV. ROBERT J., A.B., LL.B., S.T.B., J.C.D., Canonical Ante-Nuptial Promises and the Civil Law, VI-152 pp., 1934.
92. HERRERA, REV. ANTONIO PARRA, O.C.D., J.C.D., Legislacion Ecclesiastica sobra el Ayuno y la Abstinencia, XI-191 pp., 1935.
93. KENNEDY, REV. EDWIN J., J.C.D., The Special Matrimonial Process in Cases of Evident Nullity, X-165 pp., 1935.
94. MANNING, REV. JOHN J., A.B., J.C.D., Presumption of Law in Matrimonial Procedure, XI-111 pp., 1935.
95. MOEDER, REV. JOHN M., J.C.D., The Proper Bishop for Ordination and Dimissorial Letters, VII-135 pp., 1935.
96. O'MARA, REV. WILLIAM A., A.B., J.C.D., Canonical Causes for Matrimonial Dispensations, IX-155 pp., 1935.
97. REILLY, REV. PETER, J.C.D., Residence of Pastors, IX-81 pp., 1935.
98. SMITH, REV. MARINER T,. O.P., S.T.Lr., J.C.D., The Penal Law for Religious, VII-169 pp., 1935.
99. WHALEN REV. DONALD W., A.M., J.C.D., The Value of Testimonial Evidence in Matrimonal Procedure, XIII-297 pp., 1935.
100. CLEARY, REV. JOSEPH F., J.C.D., Canonical Limitations on the Alienation of Church Property, VIII-141 pp., 1936.
101. GLYNN, REV. JOHN C., J.C.D., The Promoter of Justice, XX-337 pp., 1936.
102. BRENNAN, REV. JAMES H., S.S., M.A., S.T.B., J.C.D., The Simple Convalidation of Marriage, VI-135 pp., 1937.
103. BRUNINI, REV. JOSEPH BERNARD, J.C.D., The Clerical Obligations of Canons 139 and 142, X-121 pp., 1937.
104. CONNOR, REV. MAURICE, A.B., J.C.D., The Administrative Removal of Pastors, VIII-159 pp., 1937.
105. GUILFOYLE, REV. MERLIN JOSEPH, J.C.D., Custom, XI-144 pp., 1937.

106. Hughes, Rev. James Austin, A.B., A.M., J.C.D., Witnesses in Criminal Trials of Clerics, IX-140 pp., 1937.
107. Jansen, Rev. Raymond J., A.B., S.T.L., J.C.D., Canonical Provisions for Catechetical Instruction, VII-153 pp., 1937.
108. Kealy, Rev. John James, A.B., J.C.D., The Introductory Libellus in Church Court Procedure, XI-121 pp., 1937.
109. McManus, Rev. James Edward, C.SS.R., J.C.D., The Administration of Temporal Goods in Religious Institutes, XVI-196 pp., 1937.
110. Moriarity, Rev. Eugene James, J.C.D., Oaths in Ecclesiastical Courts, X-115 pp., 1937.
111. Rainier, Rev. Eligius George, C.SS.R., J.C.D., Suspension of Clerics, XVII-249 pp., 1937.
112. Reilly, Rev. Thomas F., C.SS.R., J.C.D., Visitation of Religious, VI-195 pp., 1938.
113. Moriarity, Rev. Francis E., C.SS.R., J.C.D., The Extraordinary Absolution from Censures, XV-334 pp., 1938.
114. Connolly, Rev. Nicholas P., J.C.D., The Canonical Erection of Parishes, X-132 pp., 1938.
115. Donovan, Rev. James Joseph, J.C.D., The Pastor's Obligation in Prenuptial Investigation, XII-322 pp., 1938.
116. Harrigan, Rev. Robert J., M.A., S.T.B., J.C.D., The Radical Sanation of Invalid Marriages, VIII-208 pp., 1938.
117. Boffa, Rev. Conrad Humbert, J.C.D., Canonical Provisions for Catholic Schools, VII-211 pp., 1939.
118. Parsons, Rev. Anscar John, O.M.Cap., J.C.D., Canonical Elections, XII-236 pp., 1939.
119. Reilly, Rev. Edward Michael, A.B., J.C.D., The General Norms of Dispensation, XII-156 pp., 1939.
120. Ryan, Rev. Gerald Aloysius, A.B., J.C.D., Principles of Episcopal Jurisdiction, XII-172 pp., 1939.
121. Burton, Rev. Francis James, C.S.C., A.B., J.C.D., A Commentary on Canon 1125, X-222 pp., 1940.
122. Miaskiewicz, Rev. Francis Sigismund, J.C.D., Supplied Jurisdiction According to Canon 209, XII-340 pp., 1940.
123. Rice, Rev. Patrick William, A.B., J.C.D., Proof of Death in Prenuptial Investigation, VIII-156 pp., 1940.
124. Anglin, Rev. Thomas Francis, M.S., J.C.D., The Eucharistic Fast, VIII-183 pp., 1941.
125. Coleman, Rev. John Jerome, J.C.D., The Minister of Confirmation, VI-153 pp., 1941.
126. Downs, Rev. John Emmanuel, A.B., J.C.D., The Concept of Clerical Immunity, XI-163 pp., 1941.
127. Esswein, Rev. Anthony Albert, J.C.D., Extrajudicial Penal Powers of Ecclesiastical Superiors, X-144 pp., 1941.

128. Farrel, Rev. Benjamin Francis, M.A., S.T.L., J.C.D., The Rights and Duties of the Local Ordinary Regarding Congregations of Women Religious of Pontifical Approval, V-195 pp., 1941.
129. Feeney, Rev. Thomas John, A.B., S.T.L., J.C.D., Restitutio in Integrum, VI-169 pp., 1941.
130. Findley, Rev. Stephen William, O.S.B., A.B., J.C.D., Canonical Norms Governing the Deposition and Degradation of Clerics, XVII-279 pp., 1941.
131. Goodwine, Rev. John, A.B., S.T.L., J.C.D., The Right of the Church to Acquire Property, VIII-119 pp., 1941.
132. Heston, Rev. Edward Louis, C.S.C., PhD., S.T.D., J.C.D., The Alienation of Church Property in the United States, XII-222 pp., 1941.
133. Hogan, Rev. James John, A.B., S.T.L., J.C.D., Judicial Advocates and Procurators, XIII-200 pp., 1941.
134. Kealy, Rev. Thomas M., A.B., Litt.B., J.C.D., Dowry of Women Religious, IX-152 pp., 1941.
135. Keene, Rev. Michael James, O.S.B., J.C.D., Religious Ordinaries and Canon 198, V-164 pp., 1942.
136. Kerin, Rev. Charles A., S.S., M.A., S.T.B., J.C.D., The Privation of Christian Burial, XVI-279 pp., 1941.
137. Louis, Rev. William Francis, M.A., J.C.D., Diocesan Archives, X-101 pp., 1941.
138. McDevitt, Rev. Gilbert Joseph, A.B., J.C.D., Legitimacy and Legitimation, X-247 pp., 1941.
139. McDonough, Rev. Thomas Joseph, A.B., J.C.D., Apostolic Administrators, X-217 pp., 1941.
140. Meier, Rev. Carl Anthony, A.B., J.C.D., Penal Administrative Procedure Against Negligent Pastors, XI-240 pp., 1941.
141. Schmidt, Rev. John Rogg, A.B., J.C.D., The Principles of Authentic Interpretation in Canon 17 of the Code of Canon Law, XII-331 pp., 1941.
142. Slafkosky, Rev. Andrew Leonard, A.B., J.C.D., The Canonical Episcopal Visitation of the Diocese, X-197 pp., 1941.
143. Swoboda, Rev. Innocent Robert, O.F.M., J.C.D., Ignorance in Relation to the Imputability of Delicts, IX-271 pp., 1941.
144. Dubé, Rev. Arthur Joseph, A.B., J.C.D., The General Principles for the Reckoning of Time in Canon Law, VIII-299 pp., 1941.
145. McBride, Rev. James T., A.B., J.C.D., Incardination and Excardination of Seculars, XX-585 pp., 1941.
146. Król, Rev. John T., J.C.D., The Defendant in Ecclesiastical Trials, XII-207 pp., 1942.
147. Comyns, Rev. Joseph J., C.SS.R., A.B., J.C.D., Papal and Episcopal Administration of Church Property, XIV-155 pp., 1942.

148. BARRY, REV. GARRETT FRANCIS, O.M.I., J.C.D., Violation of the Cloister, XII-260 pp., 1942.
149. BOLDUC, REV. GATIEN, C.S.V., A.B., S.T.L., J.C.D., Les Études dans les Religions Clèricales, VIII-155 pp., 1942.
150. BOYLE, REV. DAVID JOHN, M.A., J.C.D., The Juridic Effects of Moral Certitude on Pre-Nuptial Guarantees, XII-188 pp., 1942.
151. CANAVAN, REV. WALTER JOSEPH, M.A., LITT.D., J.C.D., The Profession of Faith, XII-143 pp., 1942.
152. DESROCHERS, REV. BRUNO, A.B., PH.L., S.T.B., J.C.D., Le Premier Concile Plènier de Quebéc et le Code de Droit Canonique, XIV-186 pp., 1942.
153. DILLON, REV. ROBERT EDWARD, A.B., J.C.D., Common Law Marriage, X-148 pp., 1942.
154. DODWELL, REV. EDWARD JOHN, PH.D., S.T.B., J.C.D., The Time and Place for the Celebration of Marriage, X-156 pp., 1942.
155. DONNELLAN, REV. THOMAS ANDREW, A.B., J.C.D., The Obligation of the Missa pro Populo, VII-131 pp., 1942.
156. ELTZ, REV. LOUIS ANTHONY, A.B., J.C.L., Cooperation in Crime.
157. GASS, REV. SYLVESTER FRANCIS, M.A., J.C.D., Ecclesiastical Pensions, XI-206 pp., 1942.
158. GUINIVEN, REV. JOHN JOSEPH, C.SS.R., J.C.D., The Precept of Hearing Mass, XIV-188 pp., 1942.
159. GULCZYNSKI, REV. JOHN THEOPHILUS, J.C.D., The Desecration and Violation of Churches, X-126 pp., 1942.
160. HAMMIL, REV. JOHN LEO, M.A., J.C.D., The Obligations of the Traveler According to Canon 14, VIII-204 pp., 1942.
161. HAYDT, REV. JOHN JOSEPH, A.B., J.C.D., Reserved Benefices, XI-148 pp., 1942.
162. HUSER, REV. ROGER JOHN, O.F.M., A.B., J.C.D., The Crime of Abortion in Canon Law, XII-187 pp., 1942.
163. KEARNEY, REV. FRANCIS PATRICK, A.B., S.T.L., J.C.L., The Principles of Canon 1127.
164. LINAHEN, REV. LEO JAMES, S.T.L., J.C.D., De Absolutione Complicis In Peccato Turpi, 114 pp., 1942.
165. MCCLOSKEY, REV. JOSEPH ALOYSIUS, A.B., J.C.D., The Subject of Ecclesiastical Law According to Canon 12, XVII-246 pp., 1942.
166. O'NEIL, REV. FRANCIS JOSEPH, C.SS.R., J.C.D., The Dismissal of Religious in Temporary Vows, XIII-220 pp., 1942.
167. PRINCE, REV. JOHN EDWARD, A.B., S.T.B., J.C.D., The Diocesan Chancellor, X-136 pp., 1942.
168. RIESNER, REV. ALBERT JOSEPH, C.SS.R., J.C.D., Apostates and Fugitives from Religious Institutes, IX-168 pp., 1942.
169. STENGER, REV. JOSEPH BERNARD, J.C.D., The Mortgaging of Church Property, 186 pp., 1942.

170. WALDRON, REV. JOSEPH FRANCIS, A.B., J.C.D., The Minister of Baptism, XII-197 pp., 1942.

171. WILLETT, REV. ROBERT ALBERT, J.C.D., The Probative Value of Documents in Ecclesiastical Trials, X-124 pp., 1942.

172. WOEBER, REV. EDWARD MARTIN, M.A., J.C.D., The Interpollations, XII-161 pp., 1942.

173. BENKO, REV. MATTHEW ALOYSIUS, O.S.B., M.A., J.C.D., The Abbot *Nullius*, XV-147 pp., 1943.

174. CHRIST, REV. JOSEPH JAMES, M.A., S.T.L., J.C.D., Dispensation from Vindicative Penalties, XIII-285 pp., 1943.

175. CLANCY, REV. PATRICK M. J., O.P., A.B., S.T.LR., J.C.D., The Local Religious Superior, X-229 pp., 1943.

176. CLARKE, REV. THOMAS JAMES, J.C.D., Parish Societies, XII-147 pp., 1943.

177. CONNOLLY, REV. JOHN PATRICK, S.T.L., J.C.D., Synodal Examiners and Parish Priest Consultors, X-223 pp., 1943.

178. DRUMM, REV. WILLIAM MARTIN, A.B., J.C.L., Hospital Chaplains.

179. FLANAGAN, REV. BERNARD JOSEPH, A.B., S.T.L., J.C.D., The Canonical Erection of Religious Houses, X-147 pp., 1943.

180. KELLEHER, REV. STEPHEN JOSEPH, A.B., S.T.B., J.C.D., Discussions with non-Catholics: Canonical Legislation, X-93 pp., 1943.

181. LEWIS, REV. GORDIAN, C.P., J.C.D., Chapters in Religious Institutes, XII-169 pp., 1943.

182. MARX, REV. ADOLPH, J.C.D., The Declaration of Nullity of Marriages Contracted Outside the Church, X-151 pp., 1943.

183. MATULENAS, REV. RAYMOND ANTHONY, O.S.B., A.B., J.C.L., Communication, a Source of Privileges.

184. O'LEARY, REV. CHARLES GERARD, C.SS.R., J.C.D., Religious Dismissed After Perpetual Profession, X-213 pp., 1943.

185. POWER, REV. CORNELIUS MICHAEL, J.C.L., The Blessing of Cemeteries.

186. SHUHLER, REV. RALPH VINCENT, O.S.A., J.C.D., Privileges of Religious to Absolve and Dispense, XII-195 pp., 1943.

187. ZIOLKOWSKI, REV. THADDEUS STANISLAUS, A.B., J.C.D., The Consecration and Blessing of Churches, XII-151 pp., 1943.

188. HENEGHAN, REV. JOHN JOSEPH, S.T.D., J.C.D., The Marriages of Unworthy Catholics: Canons 1065 and 1066.

189. CARROLL, REV. COLEMAN FRANCIS, M.A., S.T.L., J.C.L., Charitable Institutions.

190. CIESLUK, REV. JOSEPH EDWARD, PH.B., S.T.L., J.C.L., National Parishes in the United States.

191. COBURN, REV. VINCENT PAUL, A.B., J.C.L., Marriages of Conscience.

192. CONNORS, REV. CHARLES PAUL, C.S.SP., A.B., J.C.L., Extra-Judicial Procurators in the Code of Canon Law.

193. COYLE, REV. PAUL RAYMOND, A.B., J.C.L., Judicial Exceptions.

194. **Fair, Rev. Bartholomew Francis, A.B., S.T.L., J.C.L., The Impediment of Abduction.**
195. **Gallagher, Rev. Thomas Raphael, O.P., A.B., S.T.Lr., J.C.L., The Examination of the Qualities of the Ordinand.**
196. **Gannon, Rev. John Mark, S.T.L., J.C.L., The Interstices Required for the Promotion to Orders.**
197. **Goldsmith, Rev. J. William, B.C.S., S.T.L., J.C.L., The Competence of Church and State over Marriage—Disputed Points.**
198. **Goodwine, Rev. Joseph Gerard, A.B., S.T.B., J.C.L., The Reception of Converts.**
199. **Kowalski, Rev. Romuald Eugene, O.F.M., A.B., J.C.L., Sustenance of Religious Houses of Regulars.**
200. **McCoy, Rev. Alan Edward, O.F.M., J.C.L., Force and Fear in Relation to Delictual Imputability and Penal Responsibility.**
201. **McDevitt, Rev. Vincent John, Ph.B., S.T.L., J.C.L., Perjury.**
202. **Martin, Rev. Thomas Owen, Ph.D., S.T.D., J.C.L., Adverse Possession, Prescription and Limitation of Actions: The Canonical "Praescriptio."**
203. **Miklosovic, Rev. Paul John, A.B., J.C.L., Attempted Marriages and Their Consequent Juridic Effects.**
204. **Mundy, Rev. Thomas Maurice, A.B., S.T.L., J.C.L., The Union of Parishes.**
205. **O'Day, Rev. John Coyle, A.B., J.C.L., The Matrimonial Impediment of Nonage.**
206. **Olalia, Rev. Alexander Ayson, S.T.L., J.C.L., A Comparative Study of the Christian Constitution of States and the Constitution of the Philippine Commonwealth.**
207. **Poisson, Rev. Pierre-Marie, C.S.C., A.B., Ph.L., ThL., J.C.L., Droits Patrimoniaux des Maisons et des Églises Religieuses.**
208. **Stadalnikas, Rev. Casimir Joseph, M.I.C., J.C.L., Reservation of Censures.**
209. **Sullivan, Rev. Eugene Henry, S.T.L., J.C.L., Proof of the Reception of the Sacraments.**
210. **Vaughan, Rev. William Edward, J.C.L., Constitutions for Diocesan Courts.**
211. **Paro, Rev. Gino, S.T.D., J.C.L., The Right of Apostolic Delegation.**
212. **Balzer, Rev. Ralph Francis, C.P., J.C.L., The Computation of Time in a Canonical Novitiate.**
213. **Dougherty, Rev. John Whelan, A.B., S.T.L., J.C.L., De Inquisitione Speciali.**
214. **Dziob, Rev. Michael Walter, J.C.L., The Sacred Congregation for the Oriental Church.**
215. **Eidenschink, Rev. John Albert, O.S.B., B.A., J.C.L., The Election of Bishops in the Letters of Pope Gregory the Great.**

216. GILL, REV. NICHOLAS, C.P., J.C.L., The Spiritual Prefect in Clerical Religious Houses of Study.
217. HYNES, REV. HARRY GERARD, S.T.L., J.C.D., The Privileges of Cardinals, XII-183 pp., 1945.
218. McDEVITT, REV. GERALD VINCENT, S.T.L., J.C.D., The Renunciation of an Ecclesiastical Office, XIV-179, pp., 1945.
219. MANNING, REV. JOSEPH LEROY, J.C.L., The Free Conferral of Offices.
220. MEYER, REV. LOUIS G., O.S.B., A.B., S.T.B., J.C.D., Alms-gathering by Religious, XII-163 pp., 1945.
221. O'DONNELL, REV. CLETUS FRANCIS, M.A., J.C.L., The Marriage of Minors.
222. PRUNSKIS, REV. JOSEPH, J.C.D., Comparative Law, Ecclesiastical and Civil, in Lithuanian Concordat, X-161 pp., 1945.
223. SWEENEY, REV. FRANCIS PATRICK, C.SS.R., J.C.D., The Reduction of Clerics to the Lay State, X-199 pp., 1945.
224. VOGELPOHL, REV. HENRY JOHN, J.C.L., The Simple Impediments to Holy Orders.
225. BROCKHAUS, REV. THOMAS AQUINAS, O.S.B., J.C.L., Religious who are known as *Conversi*.
226. GRIESE, REV. ORVILLE NICHOLAS, S.T.D., J.C.L., Marriage and the Procreation of Offspring.
227. BOUDREAUX, REV. WARREN LOUIS, J.C.L., The "*ab acatholicis nati*" of Canon 1099, § 2.
228. BOWE, REV. THOMAS JOSEPH, A.B., J.C.L., Religious Superioresses.
229. DIEDERICHS, REV. MICHAEL FERDINAND, S.C.J., J.C.L., The Jurisdiction of the Latin Ordinaries over their Oriental Subjects.
230. DINGMAN, REV. MAURICE JOHN, A.B., S.T.L., J.C.L., The Plaintiff in Contentious Trials.
231. FRISON, REV. BASIL, C.M.F., M.MUS., J.C.L., The Retroactivity of Law.
232. GALVIN, REV. WILLIAM ANTHONY, M.A., J.C.L., The Administrative Transfer of Pastors.
233. GORACY, REV. JOSEPH C., J.C.L., The Diriment Matrimonial Impediment of Major Orders.
234. HALE, REV. JOSEPH FRANCIS, M.A., S.T.L., J.C.L., The Pastor of Burial.
235. HENRY, REV. JOSEPH ARTHUR, A.B., J.C.L., The Mass and Holy Communion: Inter-Ritual Law.
236. LINENBERGER, REV. HERBERT, C.PP.S., J.C.L., The False Denunciation of an Innocent Confessor.
237. LOWRY, REV. JAMES MARTIN, A.B., J.C.L., Dispensation from Private Vows.
238. LYNCH, REV. GEORGE EDWARD, A.B., S.T.L., J.C.L., Coadjutors and Auxiliaries of Bishops.

239. LYNCH, REV. TIMOTHY, M.S.SS.T., J.C.L., Contracts between Bishops and Religious Congregations.

240. MCCLUNN, REV. JUSTIN DAVID, A.B., S.T.L., J.C.L., Administrative Recourse.

241. MCGARVEY, REV. THOMAS JOSEPH, A.B., S.T.L., J.C.L., Bination.

242. MCGRATH, REV. JAMES, A.B., J.C.L., The Privilege of the Canon.

243. MARBACH, REV. JOSEPH FRANCIS, A.B., J.C.L., Marriage Legislation for the Catholics of the Oriental Rites in the United States and Canada.

244. SHIMKUS, REV. BERNARD ALOYSIUS, A.B., J.C.L., The Determination and Transfer of Rite.

245. SMITH, REV. VINCENT MICHAEL, A.B., S.T.L., J.C.L., Ignorance Affecting Matrimonial Consent.

246. WACHTRLE, REV. PAUL ANTHONY, A.B., J.C.L., The Baptism of the Children of Non-Catholics.

www.ingramcontent.com/pod-product-compliance
Lightning Source LLC
LaVergne TN
LVHW050226080826
844660LV00012B/476

* 9 7 8 0 8 1 3 2 2 4 2 2 0 *